DISTORTIONS
OF
REALITY

"Let the fool be fooled but don't
you be the fool"

Glenn M.J. Epps

Sunrise Publishing®

Author Photo by William F. Holowka, Brampton, Ontario
Cover Design by Peanut Ent., Toronto, Ontario
First printing 1992

The author and/or publisher does not assume any responsibility for errors, inaccuracies, omissions or any inconsistency herein. Any slights of people or organizations are unintentional. Readers should consult an attorney or accountant for specific applications to their personal financial situation.

ISBN 0-9695730-0-6

Canadian Cataloguing in Publication Data
Epps, Glenn M. J. (Glenn Mitchellson John), 1966–
    Distortions of Reality

Includes index.
ISBN 0-9695730-0-6

1. Conduct of life. 2. Canada – Social conditions –
1971–   .* 3. United States – Social conditions –
1980–   . I. Title.

BJ1581.2.E66 1992   158   C92-093240-1

Printed and Bound in Canada

DISTORTIONS
OF
REALITY

A Brief Look at Each Chapter.

Chapter 1... Individuals, Society and Money

Chapter 1 deals with basic individual/societal beliefs, values and attitudes. It points out that the general morals and values of the North American society are declining thus society is 'decaying'. People in our society are addicted to many different misleading pieces of information and they do not even realize it! It is not knowing the true reality that will diminish a person's ability to achieve overall success and happiness; the uninformed person will be part of the 'decaying' society – the informed will prosper.

Various suggestions are made in this chapter and, for that matter, throughout the entire book that will help the reader achieve true and lasting overall success; all encompassing success, not just material success. Attention is also focused on the institution of marriage and the terrible issue of divorce and how a couple can help build a strong and lasting marriage.

This chapter also looks at the people with money (the elite) and those without money (the rest of the people). It looks at the privileges the money affords the rich and, simply, how the rich continually benefit at the expense of the working people.

Chapter 2...Mother Earth – Severely Neglected and Abused

Chapter 2 uncovers many 'distortions of reality' revealing 'actual reality' or simply 'the truth'. It encapsulates the problems that afflict the environment...the problems that afflict man's ability to survive on this planet.

This chapter tries to 'educate' the reader to look at vested interests such as that of the scientist. Vested interests can have a tremendously strong influence on information given to the public/society – this information in many cases is very misleading and perpetuates 'distortions of reality'.

With problems exposed, the chapter reveals ideas and ways by which the individual can take personal action to make a positive out of the negative; like the rest of the book every negative is countered with a positive.

Chapter 3...The Politics of Politics

Chapter 3 tells it like it is. Again, like the rest of the book, euphemisms are not used. The 'glamorous' shell surrounding capitalism is stripped away letting light shine on the core of capitalism – exposing it to the average person in this society. The shell is constructed by the rich, powerful and those with political clout. It is paramount that the shell surrounding the core is well-protected as it sustains the present hierarchical order; that is, the rich continuing to be rich and the rest of us continuing to be average to poor.

This chapter also looks at the role of government. It points out that government bureaucracy, size and role is out of control – government is everywhere we turn. A perspective is also given on both the United States and Canada, identifying what I believe to be areas of great political concern.

Chapter 4...Economic Crisis

Chapter 4 looks at the current economic situation and also projects the economic situation into the future. An imminent depression is forecasted for the very near future; in fact, within the next couple of years. It explains why a depression will and must happen. The only variable that exists is how bad and how long will the depression be.

This chapter also examines an individual's financial position in the economy with specific reference to investments.

Currently, many distortions exists about this subject. Many believe that they are making good investments but in 'actual reality', they are investing in what I call perverse investments. These are investments that actually reduce one's net worth rather than increasing it, as many investment advisors would have them think.

Chapter 5...Preparing for Tomorrow

Chapter 5 recognizes that the book is depicting economic and social chaos for the future. Looking to the positive, this chapter lists some basic 'survival' items that one may want to purchase in order to make the coming bad years liveable and maybe even enjoyable in some way or another.

Chapter 6...Investments

Chapter 6 is a straightforward look at some of the most common investments that most have invested in previously or currently have money invested in them, giving my opinion as to their quality in today's investment/economic climate. There is a particular focus on gold and it's potential of generating fabulous returns in the near future.

Chapter 7...The Coming Dawn

Chapter 7 will capture anybody's interest who has a intense curiosity to know what lies ahead for the United States, Canada and the World economically, socially and politically. In this chapter, I specifically discuss what I believe lies ahead for the state of the family unit in North America; what is in store for both the United States and Canada economically and socially; what I see for Europe – the up and coming world SuperPower; why I forecast that Japan 'the land of the rising sun' will soon become 'the land of the setting sun'; China the country that we pay little attention to very well may grab our full attention.

This chapter also looks at the up and coming 'New World Order'. George Bush is talking about his vision of a new world but what I see coming will be a shocker to George Bush.

Chapter 8...The Final Message

The message contained in chapter 8 can only be revealed by reading the book 'Distortions of Reality'.

In A World Gone Mad...

INTRODUCTION

Today we all create our own personal realities; realities that are more than likely completely self-serving. Actual reality is distorted and contorted over and over again. The distortions are so widespread that the distortion is now believed to be the reality while the reality is believed to be a distortion of reality. The world is absolutely upside down! Confusion, chaos and stress are just a few words that describe the world in which we live in. Traditionalists like myself are thought to be out of date and not with it. People today do whatever pleases themselves and they worry not about consequences, or others.

We live in a vastly complex world filled with many different problems, but still *marvellous opportunities abound* for those who have knowledge and foresight of future events. I am confident that this book will give you some tools to help you achieve happiness and success, to the best of your ability, given today's present societal beliefs, attitudes, and general state. Contained in this book is an array of forecasts for the future which should also help you.

Putting into practice some of the many messages and ideas in this book should help you find some 'inner peace' also known as self-actualization, a state that every individual truly deserves. Hopefully, this book will also help you achieve success, to the best of your ability, in the coming years, and for that matter for the rest of your life – a state that can be attained but the route must be learned.

Many issues in this book may challenge your present beliefs as to how to go about achieving happiness but I believe that in the long run an understanding of the truth is the only way in which an individual will be able to achieve that 'true' inner peace.

Since I deal in reality, I anticipate that some readers will view this book as being full of 'negatives'. *Negativity is simply a state of mind.* I have never in my entire life come across a negative which did not have an attached positive. Sometimes the search is not easy but the positives are there. This is a key to success. If one can recognize the positives and then recognize the positives attached to negatives, then the only direction you will head, over the long term, is up!

To get the most out of this book, I suggest that you read it when you are not pressed for time in any way. Sometimes you will need to *read slowly* or *re-read* a section. This is due to the fact that this is a highly intense book; every single line is very important. Also, this is because many of the ideas put forth in this book will go against everything you have been taught in this society and culture in which you live. You have been taught and educated by this society to see numerous issues in a particular way; you will look at things differently after reading this book. New truths will be uncovered.

I would also suggest to get the most from this book that you use personal highlighting, so that you can tailor the book to yourself; emphasizing the points that have particular meaning to you.

I came to gain my knowledge by being a social "rebel". By this, I mean that I did not follow the 'prescribed' rules and guidelines attached to the various institutions in our society. I questioned everybody and everything. I questioned the institutions of this society such as the church, the family, the school, politics, and economics. Being receptive and openminded was crucial, as many of the things you start seeing and hearing almost sound unbelievable but with a strong intensity to become in tune with reality as defined by truth and not society I came to understand that there was a whole new world within the world we live in.

You will notice that this book specifically revolves around two of the countries in North America, those being Canada and the United States. It is very important for you to also understand that the very trends that I identify and discuss, in most cases, also apply to many of the other countries of the world. Since I am a Canadian living in North America, I have an acute interest in what will happen here rather than focusing my attention on a country in which I do not live.

In the appendix of this book is a glossary of terms with appropriate definitions. Although all terms are explained in the book it might be useful to be able to flip to the definition quickly.

WHY THIS BOOK WAS WRITTEN

This book was written to help you as an individual and society as a whole attain genuine and lasting success, particularly when we are in a 'decaying' society. Most people, through no fault of their own, are misinformed or simply uninformed about many social, political, and economic issues. I have always believed that it is better to be informed than not informed; this is a basic question of ignorance versus knowledge. Often though I have found that being informed can be more stressful but one is able to make better decisions when one knows what the true picture is. The stress is produced by understanding and recognizing the many challenges that man faces. Knowing the truth identifies new challenges but one must remember that with every challenge comes the possibility of new opportunities. Today's truth is covertly hidden; this book will aid you in discovering that hidden truth.

This book has been designed to enlighten you to today's 'actual realities' or more simply 'the truth', and also the book is designed to help you cope and prosper in this society.

I truly believe that at the least anyone reading this book will say it was a definite experience and in many cases may say it has given new direction and meaning to their life!

The impetus and motivating force behind this book is 'pure'. My intent is to help any receptive individual out there to discover and learn. I am a true believer that both knowledge and experiences, of what ever nature, can lead to many positive outcomes.

** An Important Notation: I have written this book in the male tense, this should not be taken 'wrongly' by any female. It is simply the writing style that I have chosen. **

Perspectives About the Author – Points of View

Perspectives about the author is a section in which two different people from two different walks of life give their perception of myself, the author. I have put this section in the book as I think it may help give you a better understanding of the book. Knowing where a person is coming from often helps one gain a better understanding of what he is trying to convey.

These perceptions have not been edited by myself and have been placed in the book as they were given to me. I also want to point out that I did not tell any one of the people what I wanted to hear or have them say: *this would be distorting reality.*

My Perspective of the Author by Beverley M. Lehman

I feel very honoured to have been granted the opportunity to give my perspective of the "Author" of this book.

The author, Glenn Mitchellson John Epps, is my nephew. He is the only child of my only brother, John Mitchellson Wells Epps who, unfortunately met an untimely death in his twenty-seventh year when Glenn was just five years of age.

From the time that Glenn was an infant until my brother's passing, John was both father and mother to Glenn – the sad result of a broken marriage.

After his father's death, Glenn was willingly and lovingly taken into the home of my sister and brother-in-law, Shirley and Frank Miettinen and was raised by them. Even though they had two older sons of their own, they opened their hearts and home to Glenn.

By the time Glenn entered high school, it was very obvious that he had an unquenchable thirst for knowledge, an above-average level of intelligence and an extremely logical mind, as well as an aptitude for computers and an industrious nature which led to him starting up his own "world-wide" mail order computer software business at the age of fourteen. Glenn realized an unlimited amount of success from this business endeavour but, on the downside, it was taking too much time away from his studies and his academic goals which involved pursuing a university education. Therefore, he reluctantly closed down his business.

Glenn's university studies were done at Trent University in Peterborough, Ontario and he graduated with a degree in Business emphasizing Economics – subjects which have always been near and dear to Glenn's heart.

Upon graduation, Glenn entered the field of finance, specifically in banking. At this point in time, Glenn, who has just turned twenty-five years of age is in the employ of one of the major Canadian banks.

I recall with fondness, even back as far as Glenn's early high school days, having in-depth discussions with Glenn about the world's economic conditions and I always clung to every word he uttered as everything he said in this regard always made sense, not to mention the fact that, time after time, his predictions came to pass.

Today, I am proud to say that my nephew, Glenn, has just completed writing this, his first book, and has written it without ever attending a Library or any other type of Resource Centre for reference material. Everything contained within the pages of this book has come directly from the mind and memory bank of Glenn Epps.

Glenn, I wish you every success with this book and also in all of your future endeavours.

Love Always, Auntie Bev.

The first thing you notice about Glenn Epps is his determination to be the best at everything he does. Very few people have the qualities to become number one, but Glenn has an understanding of what it takes to make it to the top. I think the readers will find this out, once they start reading his book. For some people, Glenn is marching to a different drummer, but to the educated individuals who have an open mind, he is a man who recognizes societies' ills, and has solutions on how to rectify the problems.

The time and effort that the author put into the book proves that he truly is concerned about what is happening around himself and the world. Hopefully he will wake up the general population that is being trained not to disobey authority. Glenn does have the courage to speak his mind and that is good for mankind, because a lot of dilemmas are not being addressed, now maybe they will be.

If I just remember one thing about Glenn Epps it will be his intelligence. He logically approaches the issues, and is able to come up with sensible answers. Glenn certainly displays his well-thought-out ideas in the book and I expect each reader to be looking forward to his next best seller. This man has just begun, I anticipate bigger and better works from this talented individual.

Andrew Williams – Friend

I dedicate this book to the people of North America and anyone else who comes to read its message.

I cannot express enough thanks to my great friend Mary D. Wigmore, who unconditionally supported my efforts to write this book. She is a true inspiration and understands me and my motivations like no one else ever has.

Thanks Mary, Love Glenn

CONTENTS

Chapter 1 ....Individuals, Society and Money

Emotion versus Logic/The Natural State of Reality/
Institutions/Determination of Reality/Me/I;Priority Maps/
Divorce/Children As An Extension of Adults Reality/
Sex in Today's Society/Drugs, Drugs, Drugs/Who is
Conning Who?/The Injustice of Justice/Government Job –
Welfare Recipient/Welfare Recipient – Government Job/
I'll Do as I Please/Societies Blunder/The Nemesis/Society/
Awareness Programs/The Coming Cashless Society

Chapter 2 ....Mother Earth – Severely Neglected and Abused

Realities about our World's Environment/Reasons to
Worry/The Scientist, Friend or Foe?/Bankruptcies – The
Family Farm/The Truth About our Food/The Weather, A
Forecast of Danger/Changing Weather Patterns/
The Environment

Chapter 3 ....The Politics of Politics

Political Democracy/Capitalism/Redistribution of Wealth/
Government Interference/Systems of Government/
The Unrecognized Step/Family/Political-Economic
Processes/A Perspective of Two Great Countries

Chapter 4 ....Economic Crisis

The Field of Economics/The Economic Time Bomb/The
Spiral of Destruction/The Coming Economic
Depression/Corporate America Meltdown/Interest Rates/

The Worker Pays the Price/Inflation/Working Inflation/
Inflation-A Closer Look/Is There A Hidden Agenda/Father/
The Joke is on You/Earthquakes/The Secret of Depressions
Unveiled

Chapter 5............Preparing for Tomorrow

Preparing Yourself/When Chaos Hits/My Thought/
The Coming Social Depression

Chapter 6..........................Investments

A State of Deterioration/Gold As An Investment/The Dos
and Don'ts of Gold/Gold Stocks/Other Stocks/Silver/
CDs-Bonds/Loans

Chapter 7 ....The Coming Dawn

An Expert?/What Do I See For The Future?/The Family/
World Powers/A New World Order/Trends/The United
States and Canada at Crossroads/Centralized Power – The
Route To Dictatorship/A Materialistic World/Point of Sale
Gratification/The Macro The Micro

Chapter 8...................The Final Message

APPENDIX

Letter #1
Letter #2
Terms/Definitions
Index

The Search For Actual Reality Begins...

CHAPTER 1

Individuals, Society and Money

In the yesterday years, love was forever, the family was strong and happy – life was difficult but rewarding. Today we live in a society 'gone mad'. Tensions, anxieties, and stresses afflict everyone – drugs and alcohol are out of control.

Emotion versus Logic

What type of personality do you have? Are you the type to fly off the handle and let emotion be the rule of the day? Or are you the logical person separating the emotional component; or are you somewhere in between?

My advice to you is that you should certainly express emotion but do not let it interfere in your decisions or judgement processes. Try to separate the emotional from the intellectual. It is particularly important that you be logical rather than emotional when trying to uncover the many distortions of reality that are in this society. The use of rational common sense is desirable for all facets of your life such as work, marriage and investment. So many people make mistakes or overlook a critical point when they work solely on emotion. I cannot stress enough that you do some INTROSPECTION!

You must ask yourself questions and you must answer honestly. No matter what you want to hear or say, the bottom line is that you uncover true facts. Looking at the world through emotional glasses is a distortion of reality in itself. Often you will add or subtract important points just to create the reality (situation) that you as an individual desire. Looking at the world through a pair of logical glasses changes the picture immensely. You will see things other people do not see, you will think things that others do not think and you will succeed where others have failed.

Your life may improve if you see distortions that potentially would lead to your demise and make the logical/rational adjustments that are needed. A good example of this is the idea and philosophy of some people: "Live today because tomorrow might not come". This is a distortion of reality. Every day does come and only once does it not come and that is the day you die. Statistics show that the average life span is about seventy-three years old, so if you are young, or even old and feeling good, you can most likely count on tomorrow. With this distortion uncovered through your use of logical reasoning, one may become pro-active rather than reactive. What I mean by this is that you will plan for your retirement because you logically deduce that you will at some point in time, probably reach retirement age. The individual using emotion as a guide, living everyday to its fullest, will react at retirement time, not before, and this will be too late. This is just one simple example – thousands more exist.

When reading this book, it is important that you use logical rather than emotional thinking. Many issues in this book will turn on the emotional switch in you. *Try your best to turn it off and turn on the logical switch.*

Let the fool be fooled but don't you be the fool!

The Natural State of Reality

The natural state of reality is achieved when a person is able to determine what is true and untrue, what is real from that of fantasy, what is fact from fiction. The natural state of reality is more or less a utopia. It can never be truly achieved while a person is living in a place where there is constant interaction with other members in a society. The society tends to distort the natural state of reality.

At the outset, it may be controllable in the society but at its climax, you have a society so misled that the hopes of returning to a position near the natural state of reality becomes next to impossible, without going through great pains.

Today, the North American society is a long way away from the natural state of reality. Like a drug addict, the society is heavily addicted to a variety of misleading and misguided information; any dose of true reality tends to cause withdrawal symptoms, therefore only those pieces of information that perpetuate the distorted reality are acknowledged as being real. The further the society moves away from the natural state of reality, the higher the price which must be paid in order to return to a world of truth. Like the drug addict, the stronger the addiction, the harder it becomes to break away from the addiction. Coming off the drug addiction is quite painful for the addict. Society as well endures such withdrawal pains: social unrest, unemployment, high inflation, the breakdown of the family.

I believe that, at the end of the Second World War, our society was closest to the natural state of reality. War was over, global peace had been achieved, the economy was buoyant, and the family prosperous. There were other times in past decades where society was also close to the natural state of reality. Also, during those same decades the society was far away from the natural state; history seems to constantly repeat itself.

Where did things take a turn? Why are people so materialistic? Why are we so far away from the natural state of reality? The answer to this lies in the understanding of the change in the structure of our society and economy.

The Industrial Revolution was a paramount turning point. Prior to this point, society moved around the natural state of reality but no large deviations were experienced. Mass production became a reality during the industrial revolution. This signified the end of a long-standing era where people were relatively self-supportive, opening the door to a new era.

The main feature of this new era was that one left the family homestead (craft system) to take up residence in a town. The person then sought employment so that a wage could be earned in order to buy the staples of life. With the ability to produce thousands of widgets, company owners sought to create a demand for their product. The key here is create. There are hundreds of items out there that would not be saleable if it were not for the ability of advertisers hired by companies to create a demand for a product. You will find scads of these products in novelty stores. Even 'useful' products required an advertising boost in order to get the product into the mainstream marketplace.

The various forms of advertising, or more generally, media, have become a mega institution in our society and is very effective; advertising gets people buying the presented product or service. Advertising often appears to be subtle but has very strong messages directed at your sub-conscious mind. The subconscious part of your mind acts and reacts to thousands of pieces of information a day without you even being aware of it.

Some advertisement studies recognize that the world has become chaotic and exploit this. A jean commercial comes to mind immediately. You are shown two pictures, one of general stress that people face today in a big city, and the second picture of tranquillity with the man wearing a certain brand of jeans. The message to the consumer is that these jeans will bring you closer to a natural state of reality. All that you have to do is go out and *buy* them.

The secret to today's advertising is that they make it so that you do not believe that you would buy a product given the advertised scenario, but in reality thousands of people are affected by the advertising without even knowing it. The power of deception is at work!

Advertising is a tool used by businesses to actualize their need for generating a demand for their products; the underlying need is to create or increase profits. Advertising changes slowly so the people will not be aware of the change happening. Today we have advertising based upon overt sexual appeal – overt meaning an action that is not hidden. This would have been unheard of years ago. Today, it is accepted as we live in a society where sexual promiscuity is promoted. We see this in movies, commercials, books and magazines. The change in advertising took decades and is still changing.

Today we live in a complex society with an equally complex marketplace, and with it comes complex advertising. Today advertising uses every means to entice you to buy the presented products or services. Some of the brightest people in advertising are trying to outsmart you into buying their product even if you do not need it.

People have been taught, chiefly through the use of advertising, that the acquisition of material goods will bring the desired 'true' happiness. The problem with this entire situation/concept is that 'common' individuals have been pitted against 'common' individuals, trying to present the same "chic" image. While trying to present this image and look as good, if not better, than the next person, company profits soar; the advertisers have outsmarted you and their goal has been realized. This ideology has moved us further from the natural state of reality.

Don't forget who owns the companies. They are the elite of course. They are great at distorting the natural state of reality. Individuals find themselves deeply in debt and emotionally saddened while companies bask in large profits which are derived from the hard work of the societies' individuals. Corporations and their owners are rich because of you. You go to work and work hard to earn a decent income. Much of this income goes into company revenues. Without you and others like you, corporations would die.

You supposedly derive benefits from the purchased product or service, even though it has cost you money, while the corporation derives benefits through the revenues that you provide.

The company gives up nothing for its gain. Yes it does spend money to make money, but the money spent is ultimately from the consumer in the first place.

A successful corporation is a true robber of the public. Unlike Robin Hood who took from the rich to give to the poor, corporations take from the poorer to give to the richer. The corporation really is a beautiful mechanism for attaining and building wealth but does it in a perverted way. A successful company in our capitalistic society truly accommodates the state of greed.

Many people will argue that these corporations create jobs, that, in fact, they are an asset to the community. People would have you believe this reality rather than mine. Mine is closer to the truth. Corporations provide jobs when there is demand for their product and it is generally the middle and working class who create the demand through their purchases. As soon as the marketplace slows down, corporations give the boot to their staff. In other words, as long as things are good, corporations are an asset to the public – when things are bad, you had better not count on the corporate institution; it is a one way street in favour of the corporation.

Today people are chiefly chasing after material goods and our society is extremely far away from the natural state of reality. This may sound somewhat negative to some but, remember, every negative has an attached positive. Fantastic success can be achieved ... keep reading.

Institutions

Institutions are comprised of a certain school of thought. These can be moral issues, traditions, ways of behaving, guidelines of conduct, how to think of one's self in a world that has societal customs and so forth.

Institutions make up the foundation that society rests upon. These institutions help give meaning to each member's life and help each individual conceptualize his 'self'. We all come to visualize ourselves in a certain way, regardless of how other individuals see us. They help you define who you are and what your role is in society ... in life. Institutions help embrace and embody a society's culture. Since each society has a different culture, you may very well find different, new and unique institutions in the various societies around the world. There are many different traditional institutions in North America. Most are something to be proud of and something to be respected. The various institutions also generate other positive ideas, practices, and customs.

A constitution captures the institutional philosophies as a whole and provides a document that will hopefully uphold and spread its original intent. The motivation behind creating a constitution was not to create a dissatisfying or negative atmosphere for the people at large but rather to create an atmosphere that would see people prosper. Constitutions were written by traditional people with traditional views. These traditional views being embraced by Western society for *hundreds* of years. Under their guidelines, the family prospered as a unit and the nation grew as a whole. Freedoms were great but not abused or overused. Tribute was paid to the institutions – they were not shunned.

Nations that embodied such doctrines were the envy of the world. Wealth, prosperity, general happiness and leadership were but a small number of their characteristics. Those nations without any clear definition or institutional structure were for the most part substandard to the other blessed minority. These blessed nations had several different institutions with a proper mix which led to success. Western civilization continued to grow and grew on a sturdy foundation. A metaphor might better help explain this. The various institutions (such as the family, respect for others) are like the various ingredients in a cake. With the correct ingredients and the correct amount of each one you will get a good cake or a good nation. If you follow the same recipe time and time again you will get the same good cake again and again. However, change the ingredients and the next thing you know, you have a cake that not even the dog will eat, putting it bluntly.

Today, nations such as the United States, Canada and Great Britain have a calamity of people and special interest groups battering away at the various institutions that, for decades, gave our nations strength and direction; our society's foundation is being hammered away at. *Think about it!!* How many people today disregard the fundamental ideas of the church, the family, the law and so on? It is not a coincidence that the crime rate, divorce rate, and number of sexually transmitted diseases, to mention just a few, are on the increase .

There is no longer any idealized country of the world. The Statue of Liberty? Maybe once, but not anymore. That statue now stands for distortions and contradictions. Our nation and the world are increasingly becoming places filled with complex problems. When a problem arises people scurry about to hopefully find a cure. A good many of today's problems could be solved through prevention – the recognition and belief in the basic fundamental institutions of the past.

I am not naive – I do realize that everything was not perfect but the threat of divorce, AIDS, economic ruin and nuclear death would not be such a dark cloud over my life or *yours.*

Determination of Reality

For decades Western Society embodied and cherished certain ideologies, beliefs, and values. An ideology is a strong fundamental belief shared by most citizens in a society. Some of these include religion, the family unit, strong work ethics and freedom from others and government. For decades these ideologies held up, but over the last few decades the concepts and ideologies that

Western Civilization was based upon have been unraveling. Nobody knows an exact date when these ideologies began to change but I believe that it was somewhere around 1960 when we saw several fundamental shifts occurring at the same time. From approximately that time until the present, our society has been 'collapsing'. Today, we as individuals and collectively as a society, face more challenges and problems than at any other time in man's history. Today man faces monumental problems concerning the environment, the economy, societal problems, starvation...

Today, rather than following reality generated by society at large, *people create their own realities*. There is a loss of basic social congruency. It is the creation of personal realities which I believe is giving rise to this. If one does not shield himself from all the other personal realities, which is impossible, then this person comes under undue stress and strain. This gives rise to many physical and emotional problems. Take a walk through your local book store. There are **dozens** of books written on the physical/emotional problem of stress.

The societal reality that was in force prior to the sexual and 'flower child' revolution had been tried, tested and developed over decades. It was a general way of living one's life, and for the most part, it helped people gain success socially, economically, and emotionally.

It has always been my belief that, if one determined how to achieve success, one would just simply keep repeating the previous steps to success and one would continue to succeed. And, if one is succeeding, you do not radically change those steps or that recipe. We as a society have changed that recipe for success, and we are now living with it. Do you like the taste of our new concoction? *Are you on your second or third marriage? Maybe you are not able to pay the bills even though you work hard. Are you concerned about the environment? Are you worried about your children's future? Do you question the government's ability to govern? What about the increase in violence – does it concern you? Do you feel like you need a very long relaxing vacation? Is life just too fast?*

Most people today are living in a manner which is not conducive to their happiness or well being. Many people today create a reality based upon materialism in order to make themselves feel good and worthwhile. As seen earlier, the advertising/media sector has helped crystallize the idea of gaining happiness through a *shop till you drop* mentality. Society has gotten to the point where people have revolted against most of the previous ideologies. The family unit is desired but is not being achieved; religion is thought about but church attendance is down; respect for elders is almost non-existent; freedom from government interference has been totally destroyed. Society endorses the ideology of *'acquire'*, *'acquire'*, *'acquire'!!*

Me/I – Priority Maps

A priority map is simply a way of graphically showing priorities that individuals have. Priority maps can be extremely complex which is dependent on the number of priorities involved but, for the purposes of this book, I look at three different priority maps, all relatively simple. These priority maps contain only a few variables/priorities.

The Me/I priority map is the map that characterizes most of the citizens in this society. The Me/I priority map is the predominant map found in a society that is far away from the natural state of reality. The other priority map is based upon **Truth.** This becomes the more predominant map in a society that is close to the natural state of reality.

It is absolutely critical to determine what is at the nucleus or centre of the priority map. Is it the Me/I ideology or is it the **Truth** ideology? This must be determined in order for the priority rings to be constructed.

Priority rings circle around the fundamental ideology at various distances. On the priority rings are the various priorities. The priority ring closest to the nucleus has the highest level of priorities; priorities which top the list for an individual. And, logically, the priority rings further from the nucleus have lower priorities attached to them.

Priorities can move from one ring to another but the individual must exert a great deal of emotional and intellectual power/strength in order to energize issues to the different levels. The greatest amount of energy expenditure is required to move a priority away from the priority ring closest to the nucleus and also to move the farthest ring closer to the nucleus.

On the next page you can see the priority map with Me/I as the fundamental ideology.

Here it can be seen that the main priority is Me/I, as it is placed in the center of the priority map. The priority rings show that this person's main priority is career/material goods followed by marriage and family. This priority map is known as the **Perverted Priority Map.**

This priority map embodies and perpetuates 'distortions of reality'. The ability to find self-actualization (true happiness) will not be easy. If it is found, it would be due to people convincing themselves of happiness and is not likely to last over the long term. Living in a distortion of reality can only last so long. At some point in time a person is faced with 'actual reality' which can overturn the self-created happiness.

Perverted Priority Map

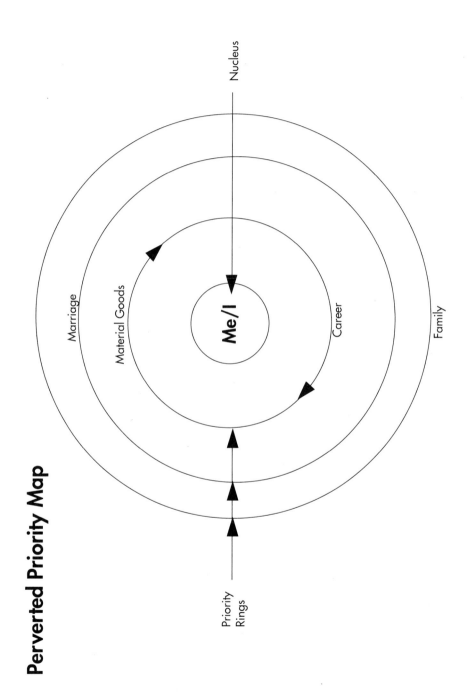

Nucleus

Marriage

Material Goods

Me/I

Career

Family

Priority
Rings

Me

Myself

and

I

Perverted Priority Map

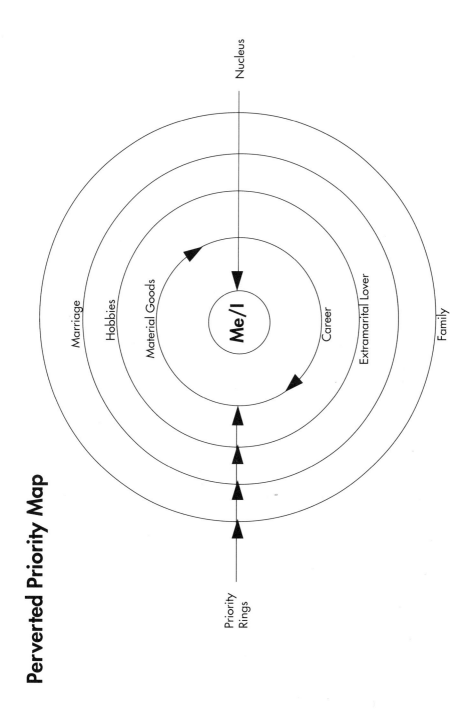

Again it can be seen (previous page) that the main priority is Me/I, as it is placed in the center of the priority map. The priority rings show that this person's main priority is career/material goods followed by hobbies/extramarital lover, and then finally followed by marriage (spouse) and family. This is another form of the perverted priority map. I have included this map as it also characterizes many people in our society.

See the next page for a completely different priority map!

Here there is a link between you and the rest of the world.

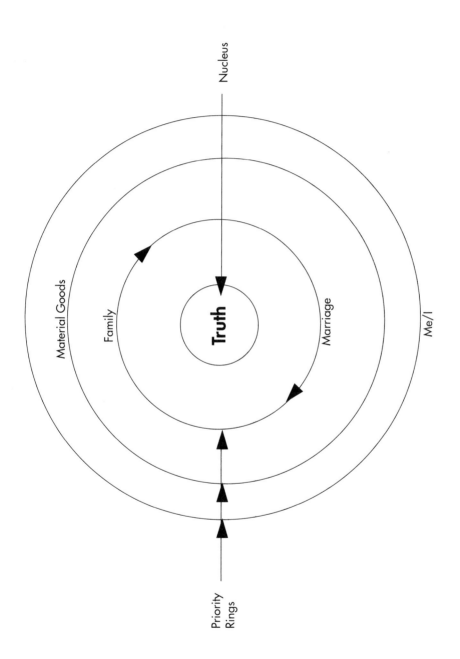

Here is a completely different arrangement. At the center of the priority map is **Truth.** Truth represents a genuine concern for others and various issues. This is directly incorporated into the person's 'living philosophy'. Putting truth at the center changes the entire reality. It can be seen that the Me/I has shifted to the furthest ring indicating that the person wants to revolve around other issues as opposed to being revolved around; this would be a fundamental break away from today's society's beliefs.

I truly believe that following this priority map will lead you to greater overall success in your life over the long run; at minimum, a better potential will be created. And, importantly, success derived from this arrangement of priorities will feel and come naturally; there will be no need to convince oneself that one is happy or is doing the right things. This is a self legitimizing priority map. You will be able to throw away all those books that tell you how to feel good about yourself.

Of course, priority maps are much more complex than the ones that are in the above diagrams. However, in order to make sense and determine priority rings along with the attached priorities it helps to break down the priority map into smaller pieces. Complexity can be managed by breaking the whole into smaller pieces, understanding, and then re-assembling.

You as an individual may want to or, in fact, you should sit down and try to construct a priority map which is a true representation of your fundamental (most important) priorities. It may take some time to do this, but it is much easier to work with a graphic representation rather than a mental picture. With a map created, you then can decide if you want to change the nucleus or move items from one priority ring to another. Even if you do not like what you have constructed, remember, you can change it. You can make yourself into the person you want to be – a person who can have unlimited happiness and success!!

**You have the right to a certain level
of Self-Determination!**

Me/I

Old folks are put in retirement or nursing homes. They are not seen as an integral part of the family unit anymore. In fact, they intrude upon the individual's ability to create a reality which is centered around the Me/I ideology. That is what is at the heart of today's reality – Me/I. People today put themselves in the center of a circle and everything else must revolve around the Me/I mentality/ideology.

Today in Canada (1990) the average household income of a single income household is $40,000.00 dollars. The average income of a two-income family is $50,000.00 dollars. That works out to $10,000.00 more if two people are working. If that family has children, then there are child care costs, loss of income tax deductions and, often, the costly expense of maintaining a second car. In reality, this average family is probably worse off financially than if only one person worked. Then there are also other factors to look at. Are the spouses of one of these families which are now typical in this society (64% are two income households as opposed to 34% just 25 years ago) spending enough time together? Are they feeding and nurturing their intimate bond or are they simply spoiling it? It seems quite clear that when you enter the institution of marriage you can not have everything. **Sacrifices must be made.** You may not be able to have the career, the family, the expensive house, the new cars, the expensive vacations, the designer clothing... This sounds like what a lot of married people are pursuing doesn't it? Those of you who believe you can have everything are probably those people who are a part of the very frightening divorce rates and have a Me/I ideology.

If you truly desire personal happiness and a marriage that will last "til death do you part", then you must look at what needs have to be accommodated in order to strengthen the marriage. This requires breaking away from strong materialistic desires and the Me/I mentality. A garden unattended will fill with weeds as will a marriage. **Do not leave things to chance – take charge!**

Many would probably agree that they do not have

enough time to share with their spouse/family, yet they still continue on in the same fashion. Their children are neglected; often raising the children is left to strangers. I have to ask why people have children if they are going to let strangers raise these children? I would argue that it is the ME/I reality which is based upon the perverted priority map. Most people have become self-centered and self-indulging. Decisions are based upon what is good for them rather than what is good for me, my spouse, and my family. The family unit, which is the most important foundation in our society, is under siege. It is no wonder that the divorce rate is out of this world.

Spouses today often miss the point that they are on the same team and should be playing together; this will ensure a better chance at success. Many married people today are on opposing teams and are clashing all the time. Today's motto is 'love thyself first' and 'thy spouse and family second'. In many cases they do not even rank second! People must realize that love begets love. What a marriage should be based upon is Agape love. Agape love is derived from Greece. Agape love is that love that is unselfish, giving, caring; giving your life for the preservation of theirs – in short the love that most seek but which evades many.

Children and teenagers today often face life alone. Mom and Dad simply are not there for them. The ten or twenty dollar bill is there for them but the caring, loving and attention is not there. Again, the Me/I mentality is at the heart of this. The children lie on a distant priority ring from the nucleus. Teen suicide in this society is on the increase. Emotional problems such as depression are striking more and more young people and at younger ages. It has been shown that a child who is raised in a loving home and is nurtured with affection through the years of one to five will have a much better chance of being emotionally stable as a child, as a youth and, ultimately, as an adult. Today many parents are not there for their children through the ages of one to five. A child care worker does not take the place of a loving mom or dad! *Do you want your children to be successful?*

If one is presently married, or is intending to become married and plans to have a family, the creation of reality should revolve around the family unit. Many probably believe that it does but some very serious and honest introspection may prove otherwise.

Divorce

So many people today become divorced, ending their childhood dreams of marrying and living happily ever after. Let me shed some more light on why I believe the divorce rate is climbing. The Me/I mentality is not the only factor involved. After talking with several couples who have been married for twenty-five years or more, I found that all of them said that there were good years and bad years. So even many years ago marriage was not always easy. There were many hurdles that needed to be jumped.

Today there are even more hurdles to jump and I believe that is why so many marriages end in divorce. The pressures of today's society are great enough to push happily married people over the edge which leads to divorce – pressures that can exist externally to the marriage – pressures created by members of this society constructing its own individual realities. Recognizing them helps you to deal with them.

Most married couples fall into the trap of today's world. They try their best to present that "chic" image which we discussed earlier. The institution of advertising plays a key role in people's pursuit of the "chic" image. They need the big home, the fancy furniture, the two new cars and a complete wardrobe of fashionable clothes for both themselves and their children. These people also strongly believe that money brings happiness. There is not a problem in having money but it does become a problem if it becomes the driving force within a person. To greatly increase the probability of success in a marriage the internal driving force must be for the cultivation and preservation of the intimate bond with one's spouse.

The average length of time staying in one job is declining as people hop from one job to another in order to enhance their career. Most people's definition of a successful career is that of making more money. Their career becomes their life not their spouse or family. This will be seen in the construction of their priority map, if of course honesty was used when constructing it. They lose sight of what brings true happiness. They overwhelmingly believe that money brings happiness; it does not. If you are not happy, then all the money in the world will not bring that permanent happiness that you desire. If you are happy, then money can potentially accentuate that happiness.

What our parents accumulated took a lifetime and a lot of hard work. Many married people have forgotten this. If you believe that hard work will not hurt you, then there is nothing to lose with this type of material acquisition. The picture is much different today. Newly married couples want what their parents have right from the beginning. What is acquired is often not through hard work, rather it is through worry and stress; many newly married couples are deeply in debt. Life is stressful enough without creating extra stress-producing situations. Everything that these couples buy is based on their combined salaries. I often wonder if these people even entertain the thought that an accident could occur, or that the economy could change, putting one of them out of work. Debt is a controller. When you are in debt you become a slave. Each month, month after month, you must make debt payments. In order to make these debt payments you must obviously earn money.

Think of what you could do if you were debt free. You may not have the same amount of material goods but you would not be a slave to the debt that you now are. Maybe you want to change jobs, but cannot because you cannot afford to be temporarily out of work. Maybe you and your wife believe that one of the two of you should be at home to raise your children but cannot afford to stay home. Going into debt today taxes your future earnings. That is, if you clear $10,000.00 dollars in Year One but spend $12,000.00 dollars in Year One you have accumulated $2,000 dollars of debt. If you again make $10,000.00 dollars in Year Two, you can not spend that entire amount as a portion of that will have to go to pay off the $2,000.00 debt of Year One. This cycle, unchecked, goes on and on until the point is reached were you can no longer purchase any goods or services because all of your income is consumed by debt payments.

In fact, if you want to increase material possessions, one should save to purchase goods rather than borrow. Borrowing incurs debt charges which do not go to purchasing any form of goods or services. In fact by putting off purchasing , in order to stay out of debt, one can purchase more goods in the future via saving. With a savings mentality you will also have accumulated interest which you can put towards your purchases. I do not want to encourage any kind of materialistic behavior but if you can not fight this kind of urge then acquire, by the best way possible – save for what you want. Debt will only create the potential for great unhappiness. At this point I would like to clarify that I see nothing wrong with wanting to have nice things. It is a problem when you live your life around getting these things. Read these last two lines again. There is a very distinct difference between them!

Children as an Extension of an Adults Reality.

The reality prevailing in this society is typically materialistic; therefore, you see children who have come to be known as "Yuppy Kids". These children usually have an expensive appearance about them. This adult extension revolves around the ME/I ideology. The parents of these "Yuppy Kids" are, in reality, more concerned with their image than that of the image of their children. Using their children as an extension to their reality helps them produce that "chic" image that they are trying to achieve and present.

The danger here is to the children on a psychological level. From day one, these kids have an identity shaped by material goods. This kind of identity is one that I believe inhibits that individual from finding or experiencing total happiness and overall success. The other issue is that it is this kind of individual who will perpetuate 'today's ways', ways that affect you and me – adversely.

Sex in Today's Society

Sex today has become too casual; there even is a movie with this title – "Casual Sex". Our society has become desensitized to it. Almost every television commercial is selling some product based upon sexual overtones; good movies must have a sex scene and you are seen as 'old fashioned' and out of touch with reality if you are still a virgin when you get married. Sex outside of marriage has become vogue; it is today's reality. Sex and sexual intimacy can be a very important factor in marriage if it is treated in a special way. Looking at sex this way will increase the marriage bond and will make the relationship stronger.

So many people today are involved in recreational sex. Again, this is based upon self-gratification. People in this society want to create their own reality which revolves solely around them – the Me/I. The general societal reality (ideology) is gone.

There are several reasons why sex should be confined to the institution of marriage. Here is one – one only needs to look at how many abortions are performed each year to women who are not married. Within the institution of marriage, if one becomes pregnant, then the chances of that baby not being wanted or the chance of that pregnancy being terminated decreases dramatically. The caring family unit fosters proper mental growth of a child. I would like to point out at this time that anyone who engages in sex and becomes pregnant but does not want to be pregnant is solely to blame. *It is generally through sheer stupidity that one gets pregnant in North America if one does not desire to become pregnant.* Even with precautions getting pregnant is possible but at least the chances are decreased dramatically.

Since engaging in sexual intercourse always has the potential for creating human life, then it should occur within the institution of marriage. It is a simple fact that human life is created at the time of conception since all the genetic material and information is completely there. All that is added biologically from that time on until death are nutrients and water. Why there are great debates on when a fetus becomes a human being is beyond me. The answer is straightforward and clear. If you believe that you are entitled to your life and that your life should be protected from the malice of others then your belief should also transcend to the unborn child. **Women have an added responsibility at caring for this life as they are the medium for growth and life of that child.**

People now say, "well, whatever makes you happy". People, unfortunately, when creating a reality which will please them, do not see that in the long run it may bring more misery to their life then they had ever expected; an unwanted pregnancy can bring many ..... and terrible ..... .

Drugs, Drugs, Drugs

We are facing a drug crisis. There is marijuana, crack, poppers, cocaine, heroin, acid and alcohol to mention a few. **Drugs are a means for people to distort their present day reality.** This reality is often harsh and cold with little room for love and caring. Many people contend that the drug problem is getting worse because more and more drugs are getting through customs; in other words the supply is up. I contend that this is not the problem at all. **Demand is the problem!**

Spending more and more money on reducing the supply of drugs getting into the country is only going to help marginally. If the state (government) is serious about tackling the drug problem then it must address the issues that create the demand for drugs. Many argue that the financial cost is too great to bear. The taxpayers cannot afford the kind of programs that need to be implemented. I strongly believe that the taxpayers cannot afford not to finance these programs. Maybe it would be better to say here that society needs to finance these programs. This would then also include the rich.

Billions of dollars are lost each year because of the drug epidemic. There are court costs, lawyers costs, doctors fees, hospital fees, lost time from work, funeral costs, and decrease in overall productivity. This is one of the most serious issues that society is facing today. These are only the financial costs. There are then the lives that are lost; the lives ruined; the families that are broken up and the pain which drug-addicted babies face.

Why is there such a demand for drugs today? Many people out there today cannot cope with the reality of their lives. Many people are faced with helplessness. They can not afford to educate themselves, they can not afford proper medical care, they can not afford decent housing and they know that this is probably what the rest of their lives will be like. They see parents and grandparents who lived the same. Impoverishment is a vicious cycle, not often broken. The 'American Dream' and the 'Canadian Dream' is just that – a dream.

Many will argue that these people have endless opportunity. After all, they live in America. This is a typical response and, in sociological terms, is called blaming the victim. Society, rather than looking inwardly and scrutinizing itself, simply blames the other parties (the poor/the victim) for the situation that they are in, even if that other party has no means to change that position in society.

The pain of this reality is often too much for the person to handle so they seek to distort their actual reality and create a myth of living on a natural high but with a high created by processed drugs.

Who is Conning Who?

The majority of corporations are owned by the rich; therefore it is the rich who are benefiting from the lavish wealth that these companies create. The present capitalistic structure is supported by the built-in ideology that if you work hard you too can be an owner of one of these corporations. In other words you, too, one day might be able to take advantage of the less well-to-do people in this society. This is then further perpetuated by those who are glorified by the media as being a rags-to-riches case. The true reality is that the odds against you becoming this successful far out weigh the odds against you staying at your present status. The club of the elite, powerful, and rich is very selective and does not often offer new memberships.

You may say that today many people are wealthy. The wealthy stated earlier is an elite group of individuals in this world. The wealth is typically old money, not new money, old money being that money which passes continually from generation to generation. Some examples of old money would be the Rockefellers, the Kennedys, and the Onassis families. The connections of old money politically is far superior than connections of new money. Power is far superior because it is so established, in fact, *legitimized.*

A false sense of prosperity is created when people see all this new money. The creation of new money over a short time span, as happened during the eighties, effectively moves society further away from the natural state of reality. Everyone wants to jump on the 'bandwagon'. People get caught up in a financial frenzy. They lose touch with reality. Look at how many television shows were on during the eighties that promoted a get-rich-quick scheme. It made some people well-off but mostly made the rich richer. The actual reality is only gained over a long period of time. Often, new money lasts only a generation or two and then is gone. There, is however, new money that does become old money – it must, however, stand the test of time.

The Injustice of Justice

The reality conveyed to society about the justice system is that it treats everyone equally and in a fair manner presuming innocence until proven guilty. This reality is simply a myth. The reality is that the justice system does not treat everyone who walks through its doors equally. The American scales of justice are often tilted to one side. The main variable in the system which greatly affects the ability to determine guilty from not guilty is money. Money, I believe, is a key element in your ability to succeed or fail in the justice system. If you have it; you can tilt the scales.

There is an indirect if not direct correlation between one's wealth and the determination of the verdict. In other words, the more money you have the higher the probability of receiving a verdict of acquittal or not guilty and, conversely, the poorer you are, the higher the probability that the verdict will be guilty of the offense or of a lesser offense.

The problem in the system is that the richer are privy to better defense attorneys; let's face it, not all lawyers are created equal. The more money you have affords you a lawyer with a higher success ratio – the ratio being that of successful defenses versus unsuccessful defenses. There was a murder case in Texas where the defendant was a billionaire. The state representatives commented that they were not able to present the same sort of case due to his ability to hire as many people as were necessary to help prove his innocence. He had more financial resources than the prosecuting state. *This present system of injustice could and **should** be changed.*

In order to make the system for which a crime has been committed against the state or society at large more equitable, everyone who enters the system should not have the ability to choose legal counsel. Legal counsel should be solely determined and allocated by the system itself. There should also be some form of random selection of defense and prosecuting attorneys. This would help eliminate the possibility of legal counsel being given based upon some personal favour or such. What a DETERRENT against committing crime this would be for the 'big boys' with the high-powered lawyers! Is that not what we as society are after – a reduction in the crime rate? It would also help assert the fact that everyone in this society is created equal, particularly in the area of law. This, of course, is not a perfect system as it does not include the ability of the lawyer (some people may still be privy to a better lawyer) but certainly seems to uphold the doctrines of the constitution much better than the present system is doing.

Such a system would be very advantageous as it would help eliminate a lot of the 'injustice of justice' found in today's system for many in society, but do not count on it ever happening, at least not yet. We come back to who is in control of this society. It is the rich and you would never see such legislation ever passed unless there comes a time when the entire society revolts against the few who control the political and economic apparatus of the country; *this time is coming*. The American scales of justice are merely a myth to hundreds of thousands of people.

Government Job – Welfare Recipient

Government jobs are the biggest welfare program ever instituted. Furthermore, the Government interferes in the free market system and is one of the most inefficient ways to transfer sums of money and provide services. I do agree that vital services such as defence, roads, education need to be provided by government but many should be left up to the private sector.

In our economy, so many people are employed directly or indirectly by the government. The government is the largest single employer of people in the workplace based upon direct and indirect creation of jobs. Working for the government means that you are being paid by the taxpayers which is synonymous to a person receiving social (welfare) assistance, with the only difference being that the welfare person does nothing yet receives benefits. Government is not known for efficiency or productivity, thus as an employer, except where needed, just does not make any sense at all.

Government needs to have as a strategic plan the privatization of as many of its departments/services as possible. The marketplace working on the premise of a profit mode would greatly increase overall productivity and efficiency in the country. Billions of dollars would be saved and could go directly to paying down the enormous national debt.

To increase efficiency, productivity and the distribution of wealth even further, I would propose that the government set up a new agency, staffed by non-political individuals, that would keep track of all the goods and services that the government would require from the private sector in order to provide those vital services. This agency then would be responsible for compiling a list of those with appropriate bid cutoff times, and making the list available to **anybody** who would care to bid for the outlined good or service. Both businesses and private individuals could subscribe to this service. This would also help bring more honesty to government by eliminating many contracts that are awarded to 'friends'.

Welfare Recipient – Government Job

What also needs to be addressed are those people on social assistance of one kind or another. We, as a civilized society, do require some form of social assistance programs, but enhancements should be made, enhancements that will benefit society at large such as described below.

The social assistance programs as they exist now are just another drain on our society's productivity. At present there is a transfer of monies from those being productive, the working people paying taxes, to those who are not working and not paying taxes. This situation needs to be addressed.

The other area which needs to be addressed is the abuse of the system. Today, just as any other day, there are people milking the system. They are there for the free ride. These people are socially irresponsible to their peers.

The answer is relatively simple. People who receive social benefits should have to work; a work for pay social assistance program. There are endless tasks to be done for the communities around the nation. I can think of several right off the top of my head such as road repair, painting, government office cleaning, grass cutting, snow shovelling... If the person does not show up for work, then there would be a direct deduction off that person's social assistance cheque. This would increase productivity and would cut down on those who want to sit at home and milk the system. For those people who legitimately need the help, it would also greatly reduce the stigma attached to social benefits. Those who truly cannot work would be excluded from having to work provided that proper medical documentation be completed.

What would single people do with their children, some people are probably asking? The answer is simple. They would drop them off at day care centres staffed by *screened* and properly trained people receiving longer term social benefits.

I'll Do As I Please

Today people say that "I have a right to do as I please, no one has the right to tell me what to do. I, by myself, will determine what is right and what is wrong". The lack of our society to explicitly determine what is in fact right and wrong is what has precipitated the great moral breakdown. Society is becoming accustomed to the "new" 70s and 80s and 90s attitudes: People today say that society has no right to dictate what they should do. A basic level of morals and values must be dictated or we, as a society, are going to face many different hardships! Note here that I have said basic level, I do not mean a ridiculous level of morals and values.

Let me explain the rationale behind my belief that we as a society do get to dictate a certain *standard level* of morals and values. The key is the Constitution, the document that our society is supposed to be governed by. The creation of the Constitution was written by only a handful of people. This small group of people dictated a "code of ethics" which every citizen has the right to. Also with the Constitution is a spirit which is the non-written words, the intentions behind the Constitution. Today people are only looking at the Constitution for what has expressly been written. The spirit is also a guideline of both morals and values. In fact much of the spirit of the Constitution carries most of these morals and values. The Founding Fathers would be shocked at the way in which we, as a society, have come to interpret such a document. I believe that the freedom of expression clause has been widely misinterpreted. I do not think that the Founding Fathers would look kindly upon any American citizen who burned the American flag. Expression is protected but not to the point of ridiculousness.

The Constitution goes well beyond just being a written document. The Constitution embodies many principles, morals, and values which together create a reality in which we as a society can live within. Unfortunately, this reality is becoming distorted. The natural reality is being replaced as society presently desires a different reality. Right at this moment, there is an attack on the spirit of the Constitution which is just as important as the written content. Slowly, special interest groups are having the spirit negated, leaving only the text to be interpreted; interpretation has never been easy but is now extremely difficult. The document that helped create a rich and beautiful country is slowly being changed through a difference in interpretation.

It is special interest groups with political clout and/or money which test the spirit through the court system. Today, judges are only interpreting what they read – the 'letter'. They all too often are neglecting the important 'spirit'. They have become afraid of acknowledging its existence. Those judges who do acknowledge spirit in the document are termed extremists, biased, and sole law-makers. They are yelled at, threatened, sent death notes, and so on. As the spirit is an integral part of the Constitution which is being neglected, the tone of the country is slowly changing. As the spirit is ignored, whilst only the written word is interpreted, our society is neglecting the true meaning of the Constitutional Document. Again a distortion is taking place.

The Constitutional spirit has become neglected as special interest groups place pressure on the judicial system to only interpret what is written and to ignore the so-called spirit. They would argue that the spirit is prejudiced to certain groups in the society; therefore, it must not be part of the interpretative procedure. That is technically correct because both the written Constitution, combined with the intended spirit does not legitimize every person/groups desires and wants. It is as straightforward and as simple as that. *Pleasing everybody is a simple distortion in itself.* So what do we do you may ask? Law making and interpretation must be based more upon a holistic approach rather than a micro approach; that is, we must make laws and interpret laws based upon the philosophy of promoting overall societal success rather than specific individual wants and desires. Every individual will benefit under the holistic approach while only specific individuals benefit under a system which tries to please everybody and every group.

Society's Blunder

The reality is that governments has been controlled by the country's society and our society has decayed. With a decaying society comes a decaying government and economy. As peoples' morals and values decrease so do those of the government. Government is a direct reflection of society.

The American government mandate is to uphold the intentions of the Constitution, Life, Liberty and the Pursuit of Happiness. It does seem that the politicians have taken this to heart. This mandate revolves around themselves and not the citizens of the country.

Canada's government's main decree is Peace, Order and Good Government. Peace and order are here, or maybe they are not, but good government? Our government's overriding mandate is good government. Would you agree that the government of today is providing good government? What kind of leadership is demonstrated?

Both countries have governments that are corrupt, governments that are not in control, governments that are essentially incompetent. A prime example of this are the Ronald Reagan years. If Mr. Reagan is being honest when he says he did not know of the Iran/Contra covert operation, then that should clearly signify to the rest of the country and to the rest of the world that Mr. Reagan was not in control of his government. Now, on the other hand, if he did know about the scandal then he was involved in criminal activity and committed perjury during the Iran/Contra hearings. Either way it was a shameful act and a disgrace to the American people. The President of the United States is supposed to be a symbol: a symbol of honesty, integrity, and morality, for the rest of the American people and the world community.

Society, or it may be better to say large segments of society, have sought out and voted for politicians that have less than questionable morals and values. Why, you ask? There has been a great rise in special interest groups over the last couple of decades. With the formation of these special interest groups, a new kind of power was formed in society. These special interest groups are not quiet and passive like a lot of the voters in society; they are aggressive and proactive. These groups sought out and supported politicians who would put forth their particular needs and wants. These needs and wants are generally not the needs and wants of society as a whole, hence the term 'special' interest groups. These groups do not care about what you want or what is good for society; they are purely interested in having their way politically. They have had great success at achieving their goals. A complacent society is to blame, a society which quietly sits back and lets others change the world without any interaction in the process. This has allowed the true political democracy to decay. Interaction will help gain back some of the lost territory.

With the fragmentation of society, by way of special interest groups, also came the decay of the political democracy as it had existed for decades. This was a result of society's members in the pursuit of individualistic realities. However, even with the general fragmentation of society into groups, society's members as a whole came to adopt a common ideology. An ideology combined with the force and power of special interest groups saw the near total collapse of genuine political attempt. By this, I mean politics that attempted to help achieve the mandates and intentions of the Constitutional documents. This common ideology was and certainly still is: government give us more and more, without making us pay for it.

Interestingly enough and certainly as expected, this can be seen as a common denominator in the Me/I priority map. The repressed emotion of pure greed was surfacing. In order for the society at large to realize their common 'greed' emotion, like that of the special interest groups, society's members sought out politicians that would satisfy/meet their desires. Politicians became intensely corrupt. Where there is demand one can be certain that a supply will be created. Society's members acted much like a spoiled child who would begin to stamp his feet but would soon stop as soon as he saw candy coming his way. In other words, so long as politicians gave in to the desires of the people, they would be able to remain in power.

The Nemesis

With a large increase in government expenditures, in order to uphold many campaign promises, did not come an equal increase in taxation revenues. This was meeting society's common ideology of, "give us more but do not dare make us pay for it all". This was achieved through a do-not-pay plan instituted by the government via borrowing. The basic reality of pay-as-you-go or purchase/pay law, was distorted. The basic fundamental principles underlying the purchase/pay law were violated. The purchase/pay law dictates that, in providing a good or service which has an attached cost, this cost must be paid for by someone and within a very reasonable time frame such as thirty days.

Here is the nemesis. The violation of the purchase/pay

law is ending; fundamental economic equilibrium is being restored. One of the economic indicators of this is the rate of bankruptcies. An increase in bankruptcies indicates that there existed a state of imbalance and that there is a move toward returning to balance or economic equilibrium.

Our society, that was on the do-not-pay plan for so many years, is now realizing that it must pay. The unfortunate part is that many people who did not receive any benefits from the do-not-pay plan will have to, in fact, pay the bill which is now due! The costs will be high economically, socially and emotionally.

With society becoming aware of the situation and politicians unable to distort to the same extent as before as they too face the nemesis, one will likely see a move by the people against politics and politicians. The spoiled child stomping his feet up and down no longer having a piece of candy being held out to him will keep stomping his feet. Then, when the child sees the adult take away the one piece of candy he had in his hand, he will throw a temper tantrum. In other words, society will no longer have more goods and services to legitimize the corruption in politics. Since the game of politics involves survival, you will no doubt see a move to politicians and political parties that have party platforms which are closer to a Truth ideology as opposed to a Me/I ideology. Unfortunately, since corruption, dishonesty, disloyalty and selfishness are the common nature of many politicians, the change that is going to occur will not be simple and straightforward. This change will add to the social chaos to come.

Society

In order for a society to continue into the future, it must ensure that the young become educated. The young must learn to do the various jobs that a society requires for existence. Society (you and I) must ensure that the young grow up to be physically fit and mentally stable. It must also ensure that the environment is protected. This can be taken even further. The human race must be able to make the environment even more hospitable as time goes on as the need for water and food, which is nutritionally balanced, increases with each new day. An elimination of both societal tension and world tension should also be present.

In effect, there is a formula for a society's success. It is as follows: Education + Health Care + Protection and Cultivation of the Environment + Stress Reducing Factors = Continuation of a SUCCESSFUL society.

For years, actually decades, our society made advances in most of these areas. That is why we saw continued upward growth in the economy, an increase in food production and family units that had strong bonds.

Today, people want to still believe that this is the general reality. I am sorry, but this reality has been becoming a myth over the last few decades. Society has lost sight of what is important. As far as I am concerned, society has taken an eighty-nine degree turn towards the acquisition of material goods.

There is hope! As an individual, you have the power and right to self-determination of your future to a certain degree. You can recognize the weak links in this society. With this recognition one can avoid just becoming one more weak link. You can change your opinion and outlook on many issues. It is not easy to reject many of the "evil" temptations of this society, but it can be done. You do not have to be sucked into this society's **black hole.** Both you and your family can opt to take a different course, a course that for decade after decade promoted general success and the continuation of the human race.

Here is a test that both you and your family members can perform. See "Personal Priorities" on page 55. Cut out fifteen pieces of blank paper, all the same size. List money on three pieces of paper, happiness on three pieces of paper and so on. Place these in front of your spouse/partner and children. Ask them to pick any five pieces of paper. If more than one money piece is picked up I would contend that this person is caught up in the materialistic mentality of this society and should read this book over again. If they are your children and are not able to read this book, you should be trying to draw their attention to one of the important messages of this book. That message is that happiness or health is not the accumulation of money.

Personal Priorities

Money	Happiness	Health	Education	True Friends
Money	Happiness	Health	Education	True Friends
Money	Happiness	Health	Education	True Friends

When choosing, be honest as it produces the best reality

Awareness Programs

Today, what would help countless people understand what our situation is, are awareness programs. Awareness programs are those programs that reveal the reality about a particular subject matter. This book is a variation of an awareness program. Other books are also good; you should seek those books that attempt to explain a subject matter. The titles of these books often contradict the conventional wisdom of our society. In other words, the book is bucking the trend and is going in a different direction than that of the majority of people in our society.

I believe that the reasons why government does not shed light on so many issues is two-fold. First, they are afraid of having mass public panic. People have been very sheltered and the truth may send our society into absolute chaos. I believe that this attitude degrades the problem solving capabilities of the citizens of this and other countries. By not sharing the problems, the government is indirectly saying that they do not have any faith in your intelligence to solve problems. Properly explained, these problems (issues) would not induce panic but would have citizens from every walk of life involved in "fixing" the apparent problems. I, personally, do not think we are at the panic stage yet, except economically. I believe we are in a very precarious position, but one that can be altered and fixed. At the panic stage change is going to be too late. At this point, I believe hundreds of millions of lives will be in jeopardy. I do believe that we will reach a panic stage if nothing is done. I also believe that this will certainly be in your lifetime if nothing is done.

Second, what troubles the government about going public with educational information is that there is the real possibility that society will turn on today's political parties. It is government after all who has had the ability over the last few decades to enact changes, changes that would be positive for both the society and the environment. This however did not happen. All too often, pressures from business, special interest groups, and even society at large has had a major bearing on political decisions.

The Coming Cashless Society

Today there is a growing movement towards a cashless society. Many bankers are in favour of it, such as Dick Thompson, Chairman of the Toronto-Dominion Bank, of Canada. With the co-operation of the banks, a cashless society is very real and very plausible before the year 2000. The banks' computers are already being linked worldwide.

There are several reasons why many people now endorse the idea of a cashless (paper currency) society. It will effectively eliminate the drug problem as no one will have cash to purchase drugs. In the new system, you will debit your account and credit someone else when purchasing any goods or services. Drug dealers will not have access, by law, to this computerized world-wide money transaction system. A cashless society will also eliminate most underground activities. Today, more and more people are dealing in cash in order to avoid the payment of income taxes and other various taxes imposed by the state. This new system will eliminate this kind of supposed tax fraud. Businesses are always looking for ways to increase profits. The cost of handling currency and cheques is very expensive. A cash-less system will cut this expense, thus increasing profits. Lastly, as our currencies continue to depreciate in value the society at large will become distrustful of paper money.

I do believe this system is on its way. **This kind of economic exchange system worries me and should worry you!** This would be a major infringement on a persons autonomy and freedom. This system would be proposed and promoted solely on its advantages; what government gives both sides of the coin? This system has disadvantages. What would happen if there was a computer error and you were deleted from the system? You would not be able to buy the staples of life. What about control? Who will be in control of this system? Frightening abuses of the system could be possible! If this system is proposed in the future, look and listen to **everything** that people are saying about this system. I would suggest that you do not endorse this system until you have a full understanding of its implications. Forget about what the government has to say – they have vested interests. Listen to the common person he will not likely have any vested interests other than looking out for other common people. Take a good look at the number being given to people. Anything *strange* about it? At this point in time what is being tested for the coming cashless society is the debit card. This card when used for the purchase of an item automatically debits your account and credits the bank account of the retailer. The only drawback with this is the problem of fraud with the card; either making or stealing them. More logically would be the implanting or 'tattooing' of this number on each individual.

Determine Actual Reality

A number graph:

```
1 4 3 4 0 9 8 3 6
7 8 1 7 8 4 0 4 5
1 2 3 6 6 6 5 8 6
0 9 4 5 2 9 3 4 6
7 7 3 6 1 0 1 8 2
```

Numbers can be important

CHAPTER 2

Mother Earth – Severely Neglected and Abused

Earth is a macro-biological experiment. Mother Earth is the host and Man is the parasite. Much like AIDS, Man is attacking Mother Earth's natural defenses which protect it from massive infection. Also, like AIDS, there is no cure in sight.

Some Cold Hard Realities (Facts) About Our World's Environment:

"The Great Lakes look and smell better than they did 20 years ago when scientists were declaring them dead but worries continue to grow that the world's largest freshwater surface is now facing its biggest threat"

– The Toronto Star

"Our beautiful planet, with which the almighty God has blessed mankind, is being subjected to brutal attacks ... No individual, State or Nation can handle the problem on its own"

– King Hussein of Jordan

Many homes in the United States have been built on toxic waste land. There seems to be heightened levels of cancer and lung diseases in these areas. Is this just a coincidence? Some lawyers like to introduce this – some lawyers have no social ethics.

The St. Lawrence Seaway in Canada is very polluted. In fact the beluga whales are dying from the toxins in the river.

Lake Ontario's fish are not safe to eat in many cases; a huge body of fresh water is extremely polluted.

The Cuyahoga River caught fire in Cleveland!

One acre of rainforest is lost to man-made fires every second!

**Lots more can be said –
need more be said?**

Reasons to Worry

Today, more people are starving than ever before. The environment is ruined in some areas while other areas are being put on the endangered environmental list. Vast amounts of plant and animal species are becoming extinct every single day; cities are choking on their own garbage, ... need I say more!

Our economic system is based upon *continuous growth* with growth leading to increased consumption. As consumption continues to increase, there is an increased depletion of the earth's natural resources. Unfortunately, many of our resources are not renewable; thus a serious dilemma exists.

We have become a disposable society. The amount of garbage produced per person, per year, is absolutely insane. This conflicts directly with the idea of preservation of the earth's environment and atmosphere. Again, the human race is faced with a dilemma.

How does the economic infrastructure continue to grow while at the same time protecting Mother Earth's environment and natural resources? No person on this earth can answer this question! The entire world order is flawed as there is no definite answer to this question. A new world order is needed and not the one constructed by George Bush. His new world order simply is a reshuffling and strengthening of power with no substance on issues that need to be immediately addressed issues that are paramount for man's survival.

Continuous consumption of the nature presented above will lead to environmental disaster. Environmental disaster will then directly challenge man's ability to sustain his own life. When and where will this madness end?

Today many people live with hope, this being absorbed subconsciously and translated into genuine conscious belief. People truly want and do believe that our scientists will come up with answers to many of man's major problems. Man creates the harmful drug, often with the help of scientists, and then turns to the scientist, a fellow man, for the antidote. Science has produced many success stories, but unfortunately, they have not kept up with man's ability to generate negative items. People thought thirty years ago that science would be able to solve all of man's problems. Essentially, science has come to be viewed as the **'God of Man'**.

The Scientist, Friend or Foe?

Science has come to be viewed as the 'God of Man'. I would assert that most people believe that the scientist is a 'friend' – an experienced intellectual who is there to help out his fellow man. It is not hard to see why most people come to view scientists in this manner. Any major science breakthrough is front page news, and there are Nobel prizes for breakthroughs in the field of science.

Unfortunately, another breed of scientist exists. These are the scientists who have developed bacterial warfare agents, drugs that have crippled children and the scientists that help legitimize the existence of uncertainty. By this, I mean the scientist who spends hours in the lab, hours preparing statistical documentations that will contravene a cautious assertion.

An example of this would be a scientist who spends hours preparing arguments to support the safety of a new drug such as thalidomide, to counter the cautious assertion by other scientists that "more testing needs to be done". This other breed of scientist has, in all probability, been hired by the drug company seeking to have its drug licensed for sale.

This must be kept in mind when analyzing any issue that involves the scientific community. *A determination of the scientists' motives and desires must be established in order to help unravel the distortion.*

Bankruptcies – The Family Farm

The family farm was often in a family for generations one generation taking over where the last left off. Farming was held in high esteem as there was that closeness between Mother Nature, the environment and man. This process of inheritance has been greatly threatened. Today, foreclosures are ending a way of life for tens of thousands. Debt loads have become unmanageable. High interest rates and low farm product prices can be blamed. Thousands of productive farmland acreage has been left untouched as banks try to find buyers for repossessed land and equipment.

The family farm and the people who farm the land should be respected and should be entitled to a fair price for their products. After all, without the farm and the farmers none of us would be eating. The ability to grow food should be treated as a national treasure. Immediate reaction and action to this situation is required in order to restore the equilibrium. We need to get farmers back into business, not deterring them due to poor economic returns. Many children of farmers today have no intentions of farming in their adult years.

A distortion has been created. The consumer goes weekly to the grocery store. Walking the aisles one sees vast amounts of food. An image of prosperity is created. The average consumer is not aware of the plight of the farmer and the family farm and is also not aware of the decreasing yields of crops and the leaching of the soil's natural nutrients. Short-term trends may have no noticeable impact, but it is the long-term trends that we need to concern ourselves with.

The Truth About our Food

Another distortion exists. We are led to believe that we are making progress – however slowly – at feeding the entire world. The truth is that the food situation is not good. Everyday, food demand increases as the population increases but food production is not increasing. The production of food is declining. You may be saying "what do you mean that the amount of food produced is declining?".

It is true and for various reasons. One reason is that our need for housing and factories is constantly consuming highly fertile pieces of land. Rather than planning for tomorrow, many builders, municipalities and governments are worrying about today, meeting present day needs and leaving the burden of worry for tomorrow's generation. Thousands of acres a year are consumed in North America. Rather than planning cities and factories on the more marginal lands, they are building right on top of some of the world's most productive and fertile land. As the world's need for food increases, society should be working very diligently at preserving the fertile lands.

Even if we in North America can satisfy our food needs, we have as human beings a moral duty to help preserve the farmlands of this continent. People born in North America are blessed with food but many countries have land that is infertile. These countries and these people have the right, as any human being born on planet earth, **to eat.** It was only through luck that you were born in this country. What would you think if you were born in India and had knowledge of how we treated the farmlands of North America? You would probably be very disgusted. We must not become so hardened and selfish that we do not try to manage the resources that we have been given in the best ways possible.

This is not just a one way deal. We also depend on others in the world for our survival. This is a relatively new concept for a lot of us living in North America. The rain forests of this world help contribute to the survival of every member on this planet. This God-given resource also must be treated with respect. Just as we have a moral duty to people in other countries, they also have the same moral duty to us.

The world, as a common human society, interlinked with the environment is a complex matrix. We all must manage our resources with respect so that the matrix may survive and grow. We may all come from different backgrounds and may be different colours and nation-alities, but we all have one main factor in common. **We are** *all of the human race.* This common denominator is forgotten by many!

On top of decreasing production, another grave problem also exists. The wonder fertilizers of yesterday are here to haunt us today and tomorrow. For years, chemical fertilizers increased the crop yields per acre of land. What studies are showing is that the overuse of these chemical fertilizers have leached out the natural nutrients in the farmland soils. Productivity is going to drop in the years to come as these chemical fertilizers continue to "sterilize" once productive farmland. Year after year, more chemical fertilizers are required to maintain the same yield. Even if the yield per acre can be maintained, studies have also shown that the nutritional value of food is decreasing. This is coming to be known as empty calories. Let's hope that we do not reach the point were one can consume food all day long yet starve to death; this is not likely, but certainly possible.

The Weather, A Forecast of Danger

You are probably aware that the earth's weather patterns are changing. The bottom line is that the human race continues to exist because of weather patterns that are and have been conducive to the growing of crops. Without crops, we would soon perish. This thought is simple but the assimilation of the idea is very difficult.

Again, as in many disciplines, there is a two-sided debate being waged by scientists. One group of scientists is suggesting that we are actually cooling down the earth's atmosphere. This is based upon the principle that, as we continue to put more pollutants into the earth's atmosphere, this causes a decrease in the amount of rays reaching the earth. This decrease in solar radiation will lead to a general cooling effect. The other school of scientists are suggesting that the earth's atmosphere is warming, commonly known as the 'greenhouse effect'. As more pollutants find their way into the earth's atmosphere they act like a thermal shield keeping the heat in rather than letting it escape into space. I am no scientist but my opinion is that the earth's atmosphere is warming up.

I believe this for a couple of different reasons, the first being that I live in Toronto, Ontario, Canada. Years ago, our winters were from early December until the middle of March. This is not the case anymore. We are lucky if we have snow for Christmas. Many Christmases in the eighties have been green. It has, on a few occasions, also rained during the months of January and February – this would be a rarity years ago, but it is not uncommon today.

I also watch the weather patterns for North America. The decade of the eighties saw summer after summer of recordbreaking heat. We can not forget about the drought of '88. Barges stranded on the Mississippi; brown-outs because of record-setting electrical demand for the operation of air conditioners; severe watering restrictions in many towns and cities; deaths due to heat stroke and a grain crop that was sizably smaller than normal. We in North America are not the only ones being affected in this way. Many locations in Europe have experienced record setting temperatures, as well as in Australia.

Ultimately, it is up to you to try and figure out what the true situation really is, but my guess would be that most of you reading this can also testify to a warming, not cooling, trend. All that I know is that we must reverse the trend whether it be warming or cooling; *both spell disaster*! The longer it is debated the more grand the problem becomes. We need action today and talk tomorrow!

Some of the best companies in the world today are successful because of their ability to change, adapt, and re-shape themselves to new and changing conditions. Our ecological environment is not static -it is dynamic. Countries of the world need to become like these successful companies results orientated. Not government studies orientated, not independent studies orientated but results orientated!

The planet upon which we live is in great jeopardy. Its health is rapidly deteriorating. We, as the human race, need to collectively take steps to ensure its survival and ultimately our survival. Collectively is a strange word to most, but we must learn its full meaning. We can no longer afford to progress at the expense of the earth if, in fact, we ever could. With today's knowledge and technologies, shouldn't our planet be getting better? After all we have super computers, we can go to the Moon, even Mars; we have cars with so many features and houses filled with various pieces of high-tech equipment yet we have an earth that is continually absorbing pollutants. We should be able to make the air better than it was, the water cleaner than it was and the land far more fertile. The earth should be respected as it is the giver of life! This statement sounds philosophical yet it is a fundamental reality. The earth with its vast amounts of natural resources has afforded man many luxuries. It is very selfish of us to continue to take without giving back; short term selfishness will alter long-term outcomes. This is a law of social behavior oblivious to most.

Man has inherited the earth and such a gift should not be taken for granted. Future generations will be greatly affected by today's actions and attitudes. The generations of the future deserve the same chances at achieving success and/or appreciating nature's beauty as did previous generations. Unfortunately, I do not know what it will take to make man see that the earth's well-being is directly related to his well-being. From my in-depth study of man's nature I do not believe that he makes changes until he is put into crisis; this is a terribly apathetic attitude yet it clearly seems to prevail. *Man is so smart yet so obtuse.* Contradictions concerning Man abound. It seems that everything is acceptable until everything becomes a disaster. Please note that acceptable does not mean desired. It is at the point of disaster that man takes serious the issues at hand.

Even if you are saying that the treatment of the environment is not acceptable, it obviously must be acceptable to countless others. Otherwise, we would see some action to clean up the mess. This seems to be a basic principle. Things are acceptable until some major action is taken against what is "supposedly acceptable" to put into effect counteractive changes. However, what is supposedly acceptable is, in reality, very much unacceptable. This may seem somewhat profound, but I believe that it is a strong component in man's way of thinking and his analysis of various issues.

Today, man's sensitivity towards the environment is very desensitized. It must become greatly amplified. The earth is not supposed to be man's biggest dump but it certainly seems as if this is the case. Each generation must deal with its waste. The cycle of passing it on must be broken once and for all! Fear that this will not happen until there is a major crisis in the world which will center around man's waste and his ability to survive. I truly hope that I am wrong. The earth cannot continue to absorb the quantities of pollutants without breaking down. Already the signs that Mother Earth is reaching the breaking point are all around us. (Refer back to: Stats about the Earth)

Changing Weather Patterns

As discussed previously, the change that we are seeing in the weather patterns greatly threatens the future output of food. The drought years of the 80s have seen production fall below consumption in some cases. Wheat is a good example. The world reserves of wheat have decreased. North America is known as the bread basket of the world. It has helped feed the entire world. The plentiful harvests are becoming less plentiful. If the production trend of the 80s continues into the 90s and even beyond, we could face massive worldwide starvation. Steps must be taken today in order to secure a prosperous reality for tomorrow.

Land management must become an important topic and not just for discussion. We cannot continue to neglect the foundations upon which the human race rests and exists. 'Distortions of reality' must be realized so that the truth may become known. *Knowledge is power; ignorance will lead to cataclysmic destruction and suffering.*

The Environment

One of the main problems that exists with regards to the environment is goal incongruence. By this, I mean that each individual has his own agenda and goals. He does not see his individual actions as contributing to worldwide environmental problems. It is only when we look at the summation of all individual actions that we see the damage that is being done. The micro makes little sense of the true picture. Micro actions seem so trivial yet are so significant. The treatment of your human waste – the micro – seems quite insignificant. The macro is the treatment of 5 billion humans' waste each and every day. **What is needed is a macro approach.** With an understanding of the macro which is becoming clearer by the day, what is now needed is to make a bonding link between the micro and the macro. This is required since we know that quantities of individual micros leads to the macro environmental problem.

Programs must be put in place which directly involve SOCIETY on an INDIVIDUAL level (the macro/micro). It's only at this point that any major steps can be made at tackling the many environmental problems that presently face this world. There must be goal congruence between the micro and macro. We, as humans, are aggressively challenging our ability to survive on this planet. Why do we not challenge our ability to find the required and needed goal congruence?

I do believe that the world population requires a world wide governing body; a new world order is required. I, at this time, would like to point out that I am strongly opposed to the New Age Movement which makes the same statements. The body which I am making reference to would make and set worldwide environmental standards. One country can no longer set its own environmental agenda as we live in a world that is dynamically connected. We belong to a one world global environment. What happens environmentally on one side of the world will eventually have effects on the inhabitants on the other side of the world. It can be seen that, if there becomes a strong belief in protecting and enhancing the environment, it is very likely and logical to assume that each individual country will relinquish its autonomy over these issues and turn it over to a worldwide governing body. In Czechoslovakia, studies have shown that only one percent of the water is clean enough to drink. I have noted that many people say that Eastern Bloc countries can simply not afford to clean up the environment. I must ask, can they afford *not* to clean it up? The answer is no they cannot afford *not* to clean it up. Priorities must be set; as of now, it seems that the environment is not a priority.

I believe that a possible solution could be that every country of the world would have to contribute a percentage of their gross national product to a worldwide clean up fund. This fund would be managed and distributed by a group of world experts, not politicians, who know the truth and they would represent all the countries in the world. What we need to see is a greatly enhanced United Nations, not only in the way of human and financial resources but also in the way of power. These experts, chosen by delegates of the United Nations, would be responsible for determining which were the world's worst environmental problems that need immediate clean-up attention.

With priorities established, money could then be allocated in order that clean-up efforts could get under way. Each citizen from the different countries must realize that we all have a very important vested interest in seeing the environment protected and cleaned up around the entire world. Stabilizing the world's environment requires that the worst environmental problems be dealt with first. Other problems can be dealt with on a priority basis.

Many scientists only agree that they disagree on many environmental issues that now face the world community. These include such issues as acid rain, the greenhouse effect, the ozone layer, the potential rise in sea levels and so on. Today, we find action delayed or displaced by studies, disagreements, and uncertainties. With action delayed, the earth slips only that much further into environmental desolation. Often today, scientists argue over the "root" causes of these environmental issues. Some argue that they do not know how much of man's actions really account for the changes that we are now seeing. It seems to me however that no scientist can firmly say that man's actions are not a factor in perhaps a much larger environmental model.

With this determined – that man does have a role to play and how little or how great that role is still up for debate immediate action should be taken. If there are more factors at work rather than just man, then, logically, I see the need to enact environmental policies worldwide regarding man's role, and to continue the studies to understand the entire model.

The great debate seems to be over man's role – how much or how little is it? If we wait to take action until we determine how much or how little, it very well may be too late; we simply will not have to worry about "how much or how little"! Let's get the environment cleaned up and we can argue for decades if need be to determine what man's role is and was.

One thing that cannot be overlooked is the fact that man's survival is directly dependent on the environment in which he lives. Practically, man should be enhancing the environment year after year to help support the continued growth of the human population. What we see happening is quite converse to this. With every year's increase in human life we see a decrease in the ability of the environment to be able to sustain this new life!

The reality is that if man does not change his ways he, at some point in the future, will begin to fight for survival on a global scale. This may sound profoundly pessimistic but we as a whole must wake up to the truth! This fight for survival will not just be limited to third world countries or countries with severe drought but will also affect countries that once had a great ability to support and nurture the growth of the human race.

If you have been having a hard time finding true meaning in your life, take up a cause. You may want to volunteer for an environmental group, you may want to start a recycling program; the choices are endless. At minimum, you should write your local and state government representative voicing your concerns, fears, and most of all, your desires. Better yet, write to your representative(s) and also send them a copy of one of the letters contained in the appendix! (See the letters at the back of the book for possible guidance). Take a stand! Doing something for yourself and for everyone else on this planet is very rewarding. Perhaps you might want to support an environmental action group such as Greenpeace. *At times Greenpeace does seem to be a little radical but when you look at the problems facing man and this earth maybe they are not radical at all.*

CHAPTER 3

The Politics of Politics

Politics is nothing more than a game. In this game, there are several players and, like in any game, the players compete to become the sole winner. The politics of our countries is a real life board game.

Political Democracy

What do the words political democracy mean to you? To most of us, they conjure up the image of a free society – a society of political privilege – a western concept that allows each voting man and woman to have a say in the politics of the country by way of the voting process. Persons who live in a political democracy feel privileged; they have some special privileges and rights that other people from other countries such as the Soviet Union do not have.

What a fallacy this is! When was the last time you were able to effect a major change through the prevailing political apparatus? Chances are that the answer would be never, or certainly, very rarely. All that the voters have is choice choice between political parties that all have the same motive – to gain control of the political machine.

A great influence on the political apparatus are the rich and the elite who are, of course, very politically active. There seems to be an apparent relationship between one's wealth and the degree to which the individual will be involved in the political process. It is, essentially, the elite who control the political parties via contributions and persuasion through their many powerful connections. There is no democracy – there is only choice amongst 'evil' parties.

I realize that the word evil is a strong one but I do believe that, for the most part, it properly characterizes the situation. Abuse of political power, corruption, political favours, politically-motivated appointments, to mention just a few does, in my mind, justify the use of evil. The misuse and abuse of political power and privilege is all around us. The choice the public has to make is trying to choose a party which will be more in tune with the middle-class people and not favouring the rich or the under-class.

Capitalism

Working capitalism, a political/economic state, in my opinion, is only slightly better than that of working socialism. I use the word working because, *in theory*, I believe that socialism is better than capitalism as it describes utopia for all members of the society, not just a few select members. Capitalism affords people a better life than socialism, such as in Russia, but is a system **designed by the rich for the rich.**

Capitalism by definition is a renewer of wealth. That means, if you are rich today and have social status, you will be in at least the same, if not a better position tomorrow – in most cases. Capitalism also says, by my definition, that if you are a member of the working-class which also includes the middle-class, you will probably be the same for the rest of your life but, at certain times, will become *less well off*. These are times of high interest rates, recessions, and depressions. .All of these are part and parcel of capitalism.

At the core of capitalism is raw greed. Greed has proven to be a more superior way of creating wealth over the years than the communist system provides. The highest percentage of working greed is found at the top of the hierarchy. The rich are able to best actualize the emotion of greed as opposed to the 'average' person. On the plus side of this, as we are told over and over again, is that we as a society do see spin-offs that are beneficial to millions of people – "It is not just the rich getting the benefits", they say. However, the reality is that the rich in making a profit of say one hundred million dollars for themselves may employ thousands of people, at an average wage, from a community. The rich enjoy the gravy whereas the 'common' person gets the leftovers, and strangely, the 'common' person is supposed to be thankful thankful that the rich created the jobs.

This notion is an important ideology of the Republican government. Both Ronald Reagan and George Bush pushed for a lowering in the capital gains tax. Doing this would greatly reduce the tax burden on the rich with a side effect of the creation of jobs for the common people. In other words, the Republican platform endorses the thought *that the rich must become richer* in order for the common individual in this society to prosper (that is, to have a job and put food on the table) – again a totally immoral and perverted ideology. I believe that we, in this society, should have the opportunity to **equally** share in wealth gains, not just a select group of people. One group of people acquiring great wealth at the expense of another group of people is called exploitation!

The Republicans believe that it is necessary to make the rich richer in order to create jobs for the common individuals in society but then endorse and reinforce the next point. In the capitalistic system, who is financially expected to pay for the government and programs of this country? If you said the middle-class, you are correct. If capitalism was as good as what most of us believe it to be, then why do the rich not pay taxes (or next to none in proportion to income and wealth) but continue to get wealthier day by day, while everybody else gets poorer and poorer even if they are working harder and longer? Capitalism is designed by the rich for the rich. It is a system totally orchestrated by the rich and solidly legitimized by the government via the political institution.

Redistribution of Wealth – The Need in a Capitalistic Society

Did you know that approximately one percent of the population own ninety percent of this country's wealth? This very elite group also knows that the only reason why this can happen is due to redistribution of wealth. The capitalist society depends on the redistribution of wealth; this is known as transfer payments. If wealth disparity was too great, the system would collapse. The capitalist society functions today because the majority of people are not poor. As wealth disparity increases so does the chances of a social revolution. As one class of people (the majority) sees another class of people getting richer through them as workers and they are becoming less well-off, chances for a revolutionist atmosphere are created. This is exactly what has been happening over the past couple of decades; that is, the rich becoming richer and the poorer becoming poorer. The rich have become extremely rich whereas the middle class have had an eroding standard of living .

The capitalist system also exists by way of the glorified dream that anybody can achieve this kind of financial and social success. The distortion of reality is that if we all work hard enough and puts our minds to work, we, too, can become rich and powerful. The reality is that this is simply not true. *Equal opportunity does not exist for everyone.* Some people are locked into lifestyles that will afford them almost no opportunities. The vast majority of the population are not wealthy and desire wealth and success just like anybody else. I do believe that the average person, if properly prepared, will have a fantastic opportunity in the near future to attain financial success. The key lies in figuring out what the puzzle of the future will look like; this is discussed throughout the book and, specifically, in the chapter, "The Coming Dawn".

It is a story about a person coming from the ghettos who builds an empire that keeps most people in the distortion – the distortion that this too can very well happen to them. The odds of this ever happening to you are slim. In other words, if you are average **today,** chances are that you will not be the Rockefellers or Kennedys of tomorrow.

Government Interference

Inefficiencies in government lead to inefficiencies in the private sector. For example, there may be a tax law change concerning pioneering company stocks in the favour of the small individual investor. However, very few small investors will ever hear about this tax law change. You may have capital tied up in, say, CD'S (certificate of deposit) – a place where many small investors keep their money. This may not be the most efficient allocation of these capital resources. If you are one of the few lucky small investors you will be aware of the tax law change, thus allowing you to move your money to areas of greater efficiency; everyone else will be left out, as usual. It is only the people with big money that generally know when changes are being made in tax laws.

Sure, the banks invest the money that you have on deposit with them (such as your certificate of deposit – CD) but these may be in investments giving a gross return on investment of, say, fifteen percent. The allocation of your investment through pioneering growth company stocks may net a gross return of one hundred percent or more. This kind of return is not uncommon in pioneering growth companies.

This essentially is an example of a capital investment inefficiency due to government interference. Government interferes in the free marketplace, first with a tax law change and then perpetuates the distortion by not making the laws clear to society's members. The reality created by government generates large inefficiencies. Government tax laws affecting investing are so complex that only specialized experts can determine what the tax laws mean for you and I. If we are just the common individuals, then chances are we will not be able to afford this expert. By simple logic, an inefficiency is created, or can be identified, when an expert is required to make sense of a tax law that has the potential to being applicable to the majority of the citizens in a society. Here is a perfect example of where the government could promote awareness programs – programs that would 'enlighten' the general public as to the government's tax law changes affecting the small investor.

Taxes interfere in the natural operation of the open market system. Another example of the distortions that may take place due to inefficiencies in government are changes to the capital gains tax laws. Any change in the system of taxation in this area has great effects on both public and private investments. Changes to the system of taxation may simply be based upon *political criteria* rather than *long-term economic criteria*. This again causes inefficiencies or, better termed, *distortions*!

Companies, like individuals, may also put off investments in particular areas because of the government inefficiency in determining specific capital cost allowances or funding contributions (for example, loan guarantees). In Canada, there is a good example of this. It revolves around a mega oil/gas project on the east coast of Canada, the Hybernia Project. For years, companies have been gathering around the table with government. Because of the incredible amount of capital outlay needed, the companies wanted to be clear on the tax write offs allowed and government investment guarantees.

Everyone on the east coast of both Canada and the United States was gearing up for this mega-project. Small companies such as specialized diving companies were preparing for this project. They made capital outlays believing that the government was prepared to go through with the project. Then, all of a sudden, Canada's government put a temporary freeze on the project. The reasons are not certain; there is simply speculation surrounding the issue. It became unclear whether or not the government was going to proceed with the project. It does not really matter what the specific reason is it is basically because of politics. *Today's political system is filled with hidden agendas. The party in power has many commitments to many groups and various people. This greatly affects their decisions.*

Are there other areas where one can see government interference? You bet – plenty! – education, health-care, construction, medical research and development, the steel industry, the automotive industry, the lumber industry, the fishing industry, the petroleum industry... it goes on and on and on. In all of the above areas, there is government interference of one degree or another. This interference could be eliminated and should be eliminated. Certainly, one should expect a level of government involvement in these areas but it should be limited. Too much government involvement is causing a decrease in productivity. Government should be there to help **promote** increased productivity. Government simply has too many hands in the pot. I see many countries around the world on the brink of massive increases in productivity. If we do not get our act together here, we will be left behind!

Every extra 'step' beyond required steps – in going from government legislation to getting to the actual working situation is an inefficiency; this is also applicable to the corporation/company as well. Identification, analysis, followed by adjustment of the steps can provide great increases in productivity and a general decrease in operating expenses. See the next page for the diagram "The State of Affairs".

Politics + Government + Politicians = Today's Mess

    Politics
    Government
    Politicians
+ ——————————
    Today's Mess

Any way you add it, it just does not add up!

The State of Affairs

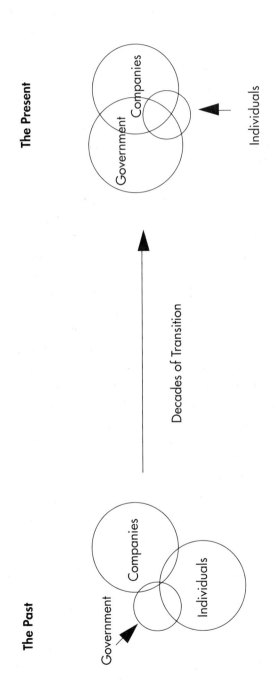

The Present

Companies

Government

Individuals

Decades of Transition

The Past

Companies

Government

Individuals

This diagram, "The State of Affairs", shows government's involvement in the marketplace, past and present, the marketplace being the social-economic-political environment in which we live – our society. In the past, government had a small role to play as shown by the small circle while companies and individuals were the main players in the marketplace. This is truly the state of democratic capitalism as described by the Founding Fathers of the Constitution.

Decades of transition slowly saw government take on a bigger and bigger role in the marketplace. Today, we have government being the major player in the marketplace with companies next, followed by individuals. Government is everywhere you turn. The individual is fighting for existence/recognition in the marketplace.

Governments should be enhancing the processes such as the protection of the environment and economic stability and growth. Often, however, their role ends up being one of interference, actually slowing down these processes. Today, the public would like the government to move rapidly on environmental issues. One example of this is the acid rain issue. Acid rain is destroying the lakes and forests of both the United States and Canada. Canada was prepared to move quickly on the issue but the United States, under President Reagan, stalled; *Reagan suggested that more studies were needed to confirm that the completed studies, which already confirmed that* **irreversible damage** *was being done to the lakes and forest of North America, were, in fact, correct.* You may be saying, yes, I know what you mean but why is government acting like this? – simply because of hidden agendas! All the time the government is talking to people – its electorate – it is in fact bowing to business (elite) interests which are quite different. In this case, protecting the environment means that companies will literally have to clean up their act; this costs money.

Businesses donate large amounts of money to campaigns and have very powerful lobby groups in Washington and Ottawa. Most high-level politicians were once businessmen themselves. I contend that business and the elite have control over the political process. You as an individual believe that you have a say in how the country is run, but in reality, you do not. You only get to choose from political parties that have their roots in business. The government acts on some pressure from the working people of the country only to help sustain the illusion of a free and open democracy. If people really understood their role in the political process and the role of businesses in the political process, there would be anarchy tomorrow. We all live in a carefully constructed reality, but, slowly, this reality is coming apart. More cracks are appearing and more daylight is shining in allowing more and more people to be enlightened. I know that, to a majority of people this will sound profound – this is simply 'actual reality'.

Systems of Government

What we see in the United States is a system of fragmentation; that is, the fragmentation of power. Often, legislation is held up for months until a general consensus can be gained. A perfect example of this is at budget time. The American government and the services that it provides can be literally shut down until consensus is reached on the Hill. This built-in fragmentation of power creates great inefficiencies .

The political system in Canada is so flawed that, during a general election, a majority of the people can vote for, say the Liberals, but, in fact, the Conservatives can win the election. Are you aware of this? This does and has happened in Canada. The system that we use is called pluralistic. We use this system because our political apparatus is based upon the Parliamentary system which was derived from England. The system becomes very inefficient – if it is ever efficient when a majority government is not elected. The reason for this is that, if the government does not hold the majority of seats, the combining of the opposition seats can overturn proposed legislation and even topple the government of the day; this can also be referred to as a lame-duck government. This is what happened with the government of Joe Clark. Upon tabling a budget, a vote of non-confidence was taken and the government was toppled.

The Founding Fathers of both the American and Canadian Constitutions worked diligently to ensure that checks and balances were built into the political system so as to ensure a society free of dictatorships or the ability of the ruling party to pass legislation that was widely unacceptable to the majority of the citizens in the country. However, they left out an important aspect. I would argue that there are only minimal checks provided on individual action. Not that I can speak for the Founding Fathers but it is my belief that they assumed that anyone who ran for political office did so because they wanted to help their country out, rather than themselves and their friends. With the Me/I ideology embraced and embodied by most politicians today, even wildly unacceptable legislation can get passed!

The Unrecognized Step-Family – Government

I would contend that the government/public sector is very inefficient. There have been different theories put forth on why this is the case but I believe it is simply due to the lack of a profit objective. The profit objective is not the best thing since sliced bread, but it does allow for an established system of measuring operating results and gross efficiency.

The government does not operate in order to make a profit. This does seem reasonable in our society. What would the electorate think and vote if the government had huge budgetary surpluses each year due to their intention to make a profit? One must not confuse budgetary surpluses with budgetary surpluses due to a profit mode. The first suggests that not all of the allocated money, through a budget, is used or spent. There may be a surplus if revenues exceeded expected revenues. Having a surplus due to direct intent to increase revenues while decreasing expenses (usually programs) would seem immoral. A government in our society is not supposed to gain wealth; its role is to provide essential services which would not normally be offered in the market economy and to re-direct and redistribute revenues (wealth) from pockets of higher income to pockets of lower income. This kind of redistribution of money is usually termed transfer payments. I also must point out that the above mentioned is theory as opposed to what truly is taking place (reality).

The Founding Fathers of both the United States and Canada envisioned governments which were like catalysts. When certain things would not get done through the private sector, the government would then step in to promote a project and then step back allowing the private sector to take over.

See the next page for the diagram "Government Effects".

Governmental Effects

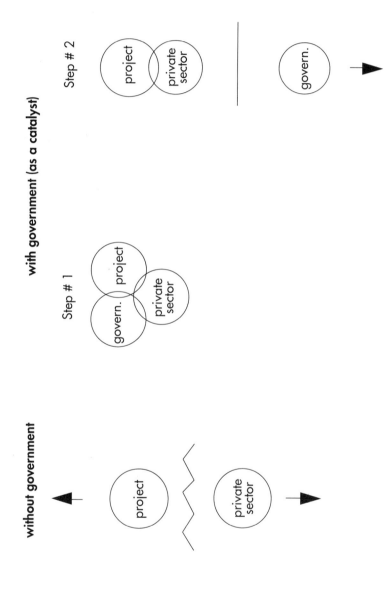

without government

with government (as a catalyst)

Step # 1

Step # 2

project

private sector

govern. project

private sector

project

private sector

govern.

The diagram, "Governmental Effects", shows us two different states – the first being a state without government intervention. In this situation, a project needs to be taken on, but will not be because the private sector is not interested. Perhaps the risk level is just too high. The second state has government acting as a catalyst. In step #1, the government acts like a catalyst generating a situation where the private sector now will take on the project that they would not touch before. This may have been accomplished via loan guarantees, grants, etc. Step #2 then shows that government now has removed itself from the project and has let the private sector take full control.

I also think that the founding fathers saw government as a checking mechanism. For example, if a company was expanding at the expense of local citizens and/or the environment, the government could step in, in order to help achieve equilibrium.

Today, in a world gone mad we have government that is involved in every facet of our lives. Interaction takes place at birth, through registration of birth, through adulthood in the way of a social insurance number, government income taxes, federal government laws, state laws, municipal laws, municipal by-laws, government forms, papers and returns and various government regulations right up till death with the government providing a death benefit. Government is everywhere you go.

The problem is that government has become so big and integrated with the domestic economy that any attempts to reduce its massive size would directly topple negatively into our economy; this also denotes a change from a true market economy, which we profess to have, to a more socialist system.

Government has changed its role from one of being a passive catalyst to one of an extreme interventionist. Our society has come 180 degrees from the time of Confederation. In the beginning years, people wanted to be left alone. People embodied the great Western ideology of the right to be left alone and the right to one's property and to do whatever one wanted to do with that property.

I know of a lady who purchased a home and wanted to attach a deck at the back – off the patio doors. She checked local building codes and found out that the deck had to be 7.44 metres from the outer edge of the property line. Her back yard was only 7.34 meters in total length. She owns the house, she pays the taxes and she cannot put a deck on her home.

Another deviation from the past is that today we have people turning and expecting the government to hold their hand through life. How many lobbyists are there in Washington? The answer is thousands! This simply says that people want a great deal from government; the job of a lobbyist is to solicit government assistance on behalf of the members of its society. The lobbyist is just as self-centered and self-indulgent as the group that hired the lobbyist.

A good example of expecting everything from government is the recent demand for a national day care program in Canada. Are you one of those people who expect the government to provide it for you ? If you are, please think about the next few sentences – *try to reason with logic rather than with emotion*. If you expect government to pay for day care for your child, then you are expecting the public to pay for day care for you; the government has no money of its own; its money is raised through the taxing of the members of our society. I then ask, "why should I have to pay for your day care desires when I had no control over the decision of you having or not having a baby"? This is basically what it boils down to. This applies to many different issues and, in fact, you may think of one that implicates me as the receiver and you as the giver. Corrective action needs to take place!

Political/Economic Processes

Did you know that President J. E. Hoover, a Republican, and Prime Minister R. B. Bennett, a Conservative, were in office at the time when the Great Depression started in 1929? Today, North America and the rest of the world, for that matter, are on the brink of financial disaster and a Republican and a Conservative, Bush and Mulroney, are in office. I do not know if it is purely coincidental or if the nature of their political ideologies/platforms set the scene, economically, for a collapse.

Both the United States and Canada, since the beginning of the early eighties, have seen unprecedented increases in government debt. Ever since the end of the Second World War, both United States and Canada have had both balanced and unbalanced budgets; however, there was never a period where the budget was unbalanced for any great length of time, except at the end of the seventies. I contend that society began to fall in the sixties but the effects were only beginning to be seen and felt in the early seventies.

Society adopted an 'I want what I am used to and even more' attitude. Since the end of the Second World War, North America has had great gains in overall productivity. These fantastic gains led to large pools of capital and profits. It was through these years that the government had no budgetary worries as the coffers were filled with more and more revenue year by year. With this increase in government revenues, there also came an increase in already pricy government programs and the introduction of many more. We, as a society, became used to these annual increases in prosperity. It was not until the late sixties that the annual increases in productivity began to decline. This was a major turning point.

Many economists warned the countries' leaders about the perils it would face if the deficits increased continuously. Society became used to what it had and did not want to make any sacrifices in their standards of living. In other words, people became selfish and greedy – only interested in today and the benefits that they may get out of that day. **The future for their children was negated.** Society set itself on a collision course with disaster! As the old saying goes, the seeds you sow today are what you will reap tomorrow. Today, society is paying a hefty price for yesterday's greed and corruption. And, tomorrow, those people will pay for today's selfishness. I, in no way, wish to imply that today's society is better; in fact, things have only worsened. We are in a world gone mad!

A Perspective on Two Great Countries, The United States and Canada

My perspective on two great countries identifies what I feel are key issues – in fact, issues that have been around since the signing of the Constitutions in the applicable countries, yet remain unresolved. The issues being the contrast between rich and poor, segregation and military power in the United States and Unity in Canada. These issues have, up until this point in time, have had a very strong political component in them. It is for this reason that I believe the issues still linger. The issues have gotten mixed up in the 'politics of politics'. I believe that it is very important for our countries to resolve these issues once and for all. I believe the way to do this is by recognizing them for what they really are; that is, social issues. With proper identification, they can be moved from the political arena to a social level. It is then up to society to see that they clearly make their intentions known to the political leaders who hold the power to make 'permanent' applicable law changes.

The United States of America

I am not an American but I want to outline what I believe to be areas that should be of concern to all Americans. In fact, not being an American will give an outsider view (bird's-eye view), which has many benefits. Often, one does not see the forest for the trees because he is so immersed in their own culture.

The United States is supposed to be a country where dreams come true, where opportunities abound and where freedom and fairness prevail. This just does not seem to be the case. There appears to be a stark contrast between the rich and poor of America. If you are well off, then that is great, but if you are poor, you better watch out because nobody else will be doing it for you.

Segregation seems to be a big issue in the United States. Many issues are always put into terms of black, white, or hispanic. Unity needs to become the key. While you sit back and decide whether there should be some sort of mixing between the all-white schools and the all-black schools, people around the world are uniting. This unity is creating new opportunities and new power. *Together you will prosper into the future; individually, you will fall as a world power*!!

I truly believe that far too much emphasis is put on military power in the United States. Your military institution is killing your country financially. The biggest military does not make the greatest country. Unity and strength of society combined with military will bring about influence and power.

The Pentagon needs to be down-sized! Funds need to be reallocated to the health and educational sectors. Equal and fair access to both of these sectors would greatly increase overall productivity. An increase in productivity translates into an increased standard of living.

My belief is that, before someone tries to clean up another person's house, theirs should be in order first.

Canada

We, as Canadians, need to get our act together! Unity is a major problem for Canadians. Quebec leads the way with wanting to leave Canada. I can certainly understand that the retention of culture is an important issue. However, this should be done by the family and individual. What is important to an individual will be passed down to their offspring.

The government is far too involved in this issue. Canada is a multi-cultural community and those cultures exist and are respected across the country. In fact, I think most Canadians enjoy it when the various cultures share their culture with the rest of us. The various cultural groups actively hold cultural events across Canada so that we may taste and experience their way of life. *The various cultures in Canada are not, however, given special status or rights as they already have the right to their cultural ways which is guaranteed by the Canadian Constitution.*

People of various cultures in Canada are proud of their culture and are also proud to be Canadian. I do not understand why a Quebecer would not like to be a Canadian. You are free to speak your language, you are free to pursue any cultural customs and, most of all, you are a **Canadian.**

Canadians are very special and lucky people. I am personally extremely proud to be a Canadian. We enjoy a beautiful standard of living. We have relatively equal and fair access to both health and educational sectors. We are respected around the world as a country that is peace-loving and which actively seeks to promote peace around the world and I, personally, believe that we, as Canadians, can enjoy such diversity in culture, especially our French part.

All of us, *as Canadians*, need to stop this bickering back and forth. This bickering back and forth is absorbing too much of the country's resources. We need to let bygones be bygones and get on with things. We need to come together to conquer the environmental and economical problems that face our country. As in the American situation, we must realize that other countries around the world are uniting. Europe is uniting twelve major cultures under one roof with less difficulty than we are having with only two. If we do not unite, we will be left behind – economically; we will be left with a nightmare. *Radical changes to the Constitution **are not needed;** changes in thought processes are what is needed*! Let's get our house in order so that we can go on to do the best at what we do best and that is promoting peace around the Globe!

Let's all work together, in our individual countries, to keep these two countries great!

CHAPTER 4

Economic Crisis

Money and material goods come to mean nothing to millions and millions of people. The field of economics and hundreds of its economists become tarnished as their conventional thinking is proven wrong. True survival becomes paramount; surviving today means life tomorrow.

The Field of Economics

Economically speaking, we are now living with high inflation and high unemployment. This economic reality is known as stagflation. This was once thought to be impossible. Economists taught students that this kind of situation was not true or achievable. This goes to show what the economists know.

Many economists are not truly economists. They simply make certain out of what is uncertain and, in the process, follow misguided principles. Now I am not knocking all economists – just most – because there are some good ones out there. I characterize myself as one of those good economists, not one who is misguided, as I do not follow misguided philosophies that have already been proven to be such.

One should be aware that economics is not a science. Many think of economics as a science. It is more an art-science and, technically, only an Arts degree is received upon graduation in this discipline. An arts-science is an arts course based in science. If any economist is reading this and is cursing my name, then I must ask you when do economists agree on anything? There is always a multitude of views floating around economic halls at any point in time. If economics was truly a defined discipline, there would not be disagreements. There would be unified concrete answers to economic questions.

Let me propose this: I believe that maths are a science and I am one hundred percent certain that you will get the same answers from others. For example, one plus one is two – you will also reach the same answer. I can remember, while attending Trent University, I had an Economics teacher tell me that the national debts of United States and Canada did not exist. He did some fancy number manipulation using mathematical principles to numerically prove his assertion. This only embedded the thought further into my mind that economics is an art. Can you imagine an economist saying that the national debt does not exist! Let me tell you he is not the only one who will say this. The national debts of the governments around the world are very real, I wish they were not but they are.

It is critical that one looks at vested interests. Vested interest(s) can have an enormous amount of bearing upon an economist's thoughts, comments, and reports. Economists working for government often have a particular view – things are not great but disaster is absolutely impossible. I have no vested interest other than promoting reality.

The Economic Time Bomb

We have reached the point of no return economically speaking. *The stage is now set for the impending depression.* I do not think that there is a chance of a depression – I believe there has to be one based upon today's economic climate, statistics and, ultimately, today's basic realities.

Many people, including well respected economists, would disagree with this and would actually say that the economy is headed for new highs, after we go through a mild correcting phase. These are people running on desperate emotion – they are distorting reality! The thought of anything else but up, probably affects them greatly. Perhaps they have a large mortgage, two car payments and all the credit cards at their limits. If you are one of these people but want to change, the opportunity still exists and, in fact, you may do exceedingly well over the next few years. *Very small investments may yield fabulous rewards.* See the investment chapter of this book.

The economy is at a point were it can not relieve financial stresses without blowing off great amounts of steam. The opportunity to turn the economy around, ensuring a future of sustained economic prosperity, was lost in the 80s. The 80s seemed to be exceedingly good years but, in reality, the financial foundation eroded terribly.

The economic policies of Ronald Reagan and Brian Mulroney have been disastrous. Through the 80s, government revenues were some of the highest in history, a good time to pay down on some of the countries' accumulated deficits through the 70s and early 80s but instead record government deficits were recorded. The 80s was not a miracle decade; this is a 'distortion of reality'. Reagan had no special genius ability to turn the economy around. In fact, quite the opposite! Personally, I believe that neither Ronald Reagan nor Brian Mulroney are intellectually capable of understanding the realities of the economies of North America. Today, George Bush, does not have a clear understanding of it either. The present economic state verifies this – what a mess. The economy was not good when their term in office began but it has only worsened under their leadership! The red ink is colossal! The government has reached a point were it now must borrow in order to pay the interest on the accumulated deficits. This cannot go on forever. There is and will be an end. The reason why the economy has not yet collapsed is due to the naivete and foolishness of a great many investors and the fact that the government is continually distorting reality. The governments of North America are guilty of generating propaganda to feed to the general public. The public is being mislead which is, of course, immoral.

See the next page for the diagram, "Government Spending".

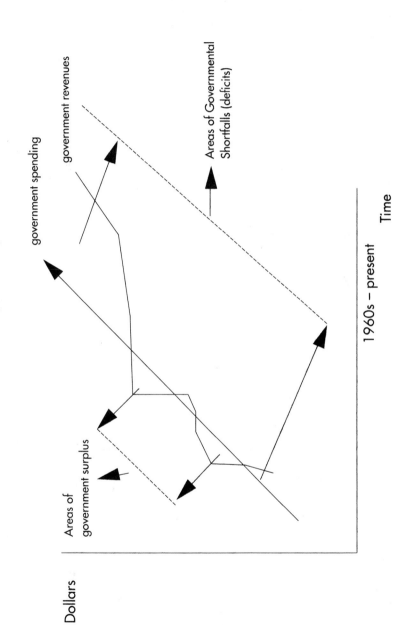

Government Spending

This diagram entitled, "Government Spending", simply shows that, up until about 1960, governments had both surpluses and deficits. However, sometime around 1960, deficits became more predominant until government reached the point where deficits have become a way of life (continual).

There is a general belief that investments in government securities is the safest place to put money. *Wrong!* Government has become nothing more than a black hole. It is sucking all savings into it and the hole only gets bigger. The money which government has borrowed will never be repaid in dollars that have any value. The spending and borrowing binge will end tragically by way of a worldwide depression.

Government has lost control of interest rates. The government no longer has the ability to set them, technically they do but, in reality, they do not. Foreign and domestic investors have the ability to set the rates. Fortunately many of the investors have not realized and capitalized on the potential power over interest rates that they do have. This naivete will not prevail indefinitely. When this realization comes to pass, we in North America can expect large increases in interest rates.

There is a reason for this ability to control interest rates. The national debt is so large that interest rates must be suitable to the investors. The government is not in a position to say take it or leave it. They desperately need the inflow of capital. Whenever there is decreased demand for government securities, by investors, interest rates must be pushed up in order to attract investors, even if it is not conducive to the economy's stability. Again, it is the case of live today and worry about tomorrow when tomorrow comes.

The government can no longer do any type of serious strategic planning. Strategic planning is long-term planning, usually over a period of several years. Today's government must constantly worry about today's interest rates, accumulated deficits and state of the economy. The management style adopted by government, at this point, is what is called crisis management. Here is the rub.

As our economies move into a deep recession government revenues will decrease due to a loss in taxes caused by decreases in consumption and income. At the same time, government expenses will rise, due to increased costs of various social programs such as unemployment insurance, social assistance, retraining expenses, ect. This will dictate that the government borrow even more. The government will be trying to manage another economic crisis as well. As the recession worsens, the need for cash (capital) will increase dramatically. In order to attract investors to government securities interest rates will have to rise. A rise in interest rates will only de-stabilize the economy further. This is the spiral of destruction.

The Spiral of Destruction

One of the main funders of our debt are the Japanese. The Japanese, if they look at the situation logically, will see their terrible predicament – revered today as one of the worlds foremost financial leaders and innovators – criticized tomorrow, internally, for not having recognized their poor investment decisions/choices. Essentially the Japanese will have lost to the Americans twice in the 20th century. The Japanese have invested so much, and even if they realize that the debt can never be repaid, they cannot stop lending. It is a catch 22! The minute the lending stops, the world will face a very destructive financial depression. Their only choice is to move the day of reckoning forward in time. This is moved forward by continuing to fund the deficits of North America. They will be distorting reality in the same manner that we in North America have.

The Japanese are going to face large losses of foreign investments in the future. I believe that it will be more than just financial assets, such as stocks and treasury bills, that they will lose. They own vast amounts of real estate in the United States and I believe they will lose it through nationalization by the United States government.

You may ask "why are more people not aware of this" –

why are the informed not telling the public the true state of affairs? Well many people do know and they are trying to warn the public. But many people are not receptive to this kind of doom-saying – it does not fit into their reality which is a distortion of actual reality. They need and want to hear that everything is stable and that further prosperity is down the road – in fact, just around the corner. Many citizens are going to be in for a rude awakening. Would you not rather know the truth and prepare yourself for tomorrow? Problems can not be adequately dealt with unless the truth is known. Or would you prefer to go on, living in a myth.? The first is the logical choice, the second is based upon emotional reasoning. *As I have said earlier, emotional reasoning only increases the probability of ending any situation in tragedy; whereas, logical reasoning increases the chances of having positive outcomes.*

The Coming Economic Depression

Yes, a world wide economic depression is imminent. By the time you read this book we already may be in a depression. While a junior in High School, I forecasted a depression around the years 1988 or 1989. I see that I am slightly off but still stand behind my original forecast of a world-wide depression. I underestimated the government's ability to distort reality. I should have known better; after all, they are politicians.

The depression will be like no other! Many depressions of the past have been labelled the great depression, but this next depression will be the greatest depression that the world has ever seen. The reason why this depression will make all previous depressions look like recessions is that our world has become a highly integrated global economy. Every country is inter-linked with the rest. It is basically a set of dominos waiting to be triggered. What happens in Japan affects us on the other side of the globe and, conversely, what happens in North America affects the rest of the world.

Even the poorest of nations, the Third World countries, can affect our way of life by the fact that they, at any time, could announce that they will not pay back the billions and billions of dollars that have been lent to them; this day is coming. Again, every country on this earth can impact the world economy in some way or another.

Today, many economists argue that we will never have another depression like that of the 1930s. They assert that we simply have too many built in 'safety features' which will prevent such a meltdown. I agree that the next depression will not be like that of the 1930s – it will be much worse! Who are they trying to kid? The basic fundamentals derived from Keynesian economics as safety features for the economy, have been violated. One of the most important concepts, that of balancing a budget during economically prosperous years, has been violated. The premise behind this is than when an economic downturn takes place, the government can borrow money to finance various 'safety feature' programs in order to inject money into the economy when it is most needed.

Depressions have always plagued the world and this modern society has not yet figured out how to avoid a simple recession, let alone a depression. Governments are always introducing legislation which will supposedly combat high unemployment, high inflation, and the threat of a recession. Anyone who is more than eight years old has lived through at least one recession – maybe several – and even possibly the great depression of the thirties.

There are several factors that contribute to the coming depression.

(1) High levels of government debt.
The debt owed is so great that it will never be repaid and is slowly choking the economy by requiring such large amounts of capital just to service the interest payments. The American and Canadian governments are now borrowing to pay interest. One can see that we, in the first world,

actually are not in a much better position, debt wise, than those in the third world.

(2) **Persistent levels of inflation of one to two per cent.**

Inflation is eating away at productivity and away at the middle-class way of life. More and more money is being earned, but in terms of purchasing power it has been on the downward slide for almost two decades.

(3) **High levels of personal debt.**

Consumer debt today is at record levels. More and more of a person's disposable income is being channelled to servicing of debt rather than being used to purchase goods and services in this society.

(4) **Overvalued Stocks**

The larger a speculative bubble grows -the larger the correction needs to be. Speculation does not go unchecked for ad infinitum. Many stocks today are still overvalued. Price to earnings ratios are ridiculously high. We see the Dow still at relatively high levels in relation to previous past averages and in light of poor corporate profits, a persistent trade imbalance in the United States and also high levels of both inflation and interest rates.

(5) **Real estate in many areas is grossly overpriced.**

As this speculative bubble bursts, one will see further deterioration in the banking sector as people will simply walk away from their mortgages. Lets assume that you bought a $100 000.00 dollar home and put down 10% this leaves you with a $90 000.00 dollar mortgage. Now assuming that house prices fall by 15% your home is not worth $85 000.00 dollars yet you are trying to pay off a $90 000.00 dollar mortgage. In this scenario, continuing to make mortgage payments is simply not logical. A 15% drop in prices is certainly not unrealistic. During the depression of the thirties many homes and land values dropped by more than 75%!

(6) Corporate America is Heavily Burdened with Debt.
The speculative merger mania of the eighties era can be blamed for this. Many companies' appraised worths have been grossly over-valued and thus carry a heavy load of debt. One company would borrow heavily in order to acquire the overpriced corporation. These companies with high debts require an extremely large cash flow. When the financing was arranged for these take-overs, most of the financial projections were for continued and sustained growth which is absolutely unrealistic. This is not reality. This is a distorted reality; however, everyone knows that, sooner or later, the growth rate will decrease if not become negative. This, in a great many cases, was simply not factored properly into the financial projections. As the economy of North America now slows down, many companies are starting to face debt payments which are becoming harder and harder to make. This only reinforces the point that the financial projections for these companies were inaccurately calculated.

Corporate America Meltdown

The backbone behind our capitalist society is corporate America. I see this whole sector coming unraveled in the coming depression. In fact, I think it will be so bad that after it is over, we may not see capitalism as we know it ever again. Before corporate America becomes a wasteland I believe that the government will try desperately to prop them up through grants, loans and loan guarantees. This will only add to the nation's inflationary problems.

It is at this point that you probably will see inflation really kicking up, and the general public will become alarmed at the inflation rate and will start dumping their dollars for any sort of tangible assets. Capitalism will be questioned by the general public; corporate America will be questioned. The pain and hardship will be so great that everyone will be receptive to a new way of life – a new world order. What this new order will be I cannot exactly say but it seems reasonable to expect a mix between communism and capitalism, uniting the positive qualities of each and excluding as many of the negative qualities of each, as possible.

There will be tremendous jealousy still in the system as people will still see rich people living the 'good life' while they are fighting for basic survival. This will spark a major redistribution of wealth, a global political initiative something that capitalism would never endorse.

Interest Rates

As a recession sinks in across the world, the group of seven advanced industrial countries/societies, I expect, will collaborate in order to reduce interest rates as they did after the stock market crash of 1987. This kind of measure will only work if economic conditions worsen only slightly. In a major depression, the political pressures at home are just far too great for there to be any type of worldwide financial policies. It basically boils down to every country for itself. When people in one nation (a society) are desperate, they are not interested in helping another nation (society); they simply want to improve their individual situation. This seems cold but this is basic human nature – survival.

An all-out worldwide depression will put tremendous downward pressures on many currencies – particularly the United States dollar and this will cause an upward surge in interest rates. This increase in interest rates strengthens the dollar by attracting capital inflows. A selfish attitude will overcome the individual countries, trying their best to protect their country and its people. What you will see is an all-out interest rate war by the various countries. In times of crisis, governments act in total defense of their currency and, with it, the maintenance of social stability. One interest rate increase in one country will spark another interest rate increase in another and so on and so on.

The Worker 'Pays' the Price

Workers today, as in the past, have been expected to take the brunt of inflation. Wage demands are one of the top priorities of unions and individual workers around North America. Working people want to have their salaries keep up with inflation. As inflation rises a majority of the burden is put on the backs of workers via a drop in wage increases. Interest rates are pushed up which in turn slows down the economy, making unemployment rise. As unemployment rises, wage hike pressures reduce as workers get weary of the potential of job loss.

Workers are asked to take increases that often do not keep up with inflation; workers often accept packages like this because they are told that they may lose their jobs if concessions are not made. **What this is saying is that workers cannot share in the capital growth of the country; I have a problem with this ideology – do you?**

Wages, to a certain extent, do cause some inflationary pressures, but there are many other factors that make up the inflation picture.

Inflation

Inflation is a very important issue but so many people do not understand it. Inflation affects everyone; therefore, everyone should have an understanding of it. This can be blamed on the government and the educational system. They have done nothing to explain inflation; however, they, the acting government, have often said that wage demands are to blame for the nation's inflationary problems. They implicate most people as being a part of the problem but do not explain the entire situation. This is simply misleading and immoral. If one is implicated as being part of a problem, then that individual has a right to understand the entire issue.

A simple definition of inflation is that too much money is chasing too few goods. To better explain this, let me give you a simple example. Let's say we have a simple economy of two people and one good to buy – both people have five dollars to spend and the product has a price tag of five dollars – if only one person wants the product, then the price would be five dollars. Now let's suppose that both people want the product and we give them an extra five dollars each (a wage increase). The product, theoretically, could sell for ten dollars now, since both people have ten dollars to spend. This is too much money chasing too few goods. Now if there were two of the products to buy, then the price could drop down to the original price of five dollars per unit. Inflation, of course, is much more complex than this. It embodies many factors such as wage demands, interest rates, government spending, corporate spending, personal spending, printing of money, government debt, the loss of faith in fiat currency, to mention just a few of the various factors. There are many more factors involved. The reality is that the inflation model is so complex that no one individual or organization has ever come to fully understand it. If it was fully understood, it would only make sense to me that it would be eliminated in our economy; inflation has always been a part of our economy.

Inflation eats away at savings, reduces returns on investments, and pushes prices up. Inflation is like radiation. You do not physically feel or directly see inflation but it is real and does terrible damage, even permanent damage to a country's well being and to individuals as well.

Working Inflation

Let me use a couple of examples to show you how inflation works and also why inflation is a terrible evil.

Let's suppose you have one thousand dollars to invest, the rate of return you get is twelve percent, inflation is at four percent and you are in a thirty per cent tax bracket.

note that a bracket indicates monies owing or lost

1000 x .12 = $120 interest earned on investment
1000 x .04 = $(40) inflation factor
120 x .30 = $(36) taxes owing

120–40–36 = $44

Due to inflation and taxation you have actually made only 4.4% on your money, not the advertised 12% This 4.4% rate of return on your money is what is called the real rate of return. A real rate of return factors in inflation.

Now let us change the scenario. Assume that you have the same one thousand dollars, rate of return is twelve percent, and the inflation rate is ten percent.

1000 x .12 = $120 interest earned on investment
1000 x .10 = $(100) inflation factor
120 x .30 = $(36) taxes owing

120–100–36 = –$(14)

Due to inflation and taxation you have actually lost money! You have made one hundred and twenty dollars via the investment but have lost one hundred in purchasing power and paid thirty six dollars in taxes. Your income (net worth) has actually declined by fourteen dollars! Just think of it if you had fifty thousand dollars invested in this kind of scenario. You would have lost fourteen dollars per thousand or seven hundred dollars. By investing, you have actually lost money.

Some readers may be saying, well, this is just a hypothetical situation and if inflation goes up so do interest rates paid on investments. Yes, this is true, but think about how many people have fixed-term investments. Many people have investments locked in for up to five years. When the original investment was taken out it may have looked good but economically-speaking, things can change quickly. Many people were in this situation in the seventies and early eighties. At this point, many readers may be asking what, then, should a person invest in. This will be discussed in the investment chapter of the book.

Let's get back to why the government does not help people understand inflation or why any investing firm does not help you understand. It is for the simple reason that there would be chaos. There are many of these **Perverse Investments** out there. *A perverse investment is any investment that costs you more than the real rate of return on the investment.* You must shop around to find investments that are not perverse or investments that are designed to cope with a dynamic investment/economic environment. If everyone learned the actual reality, there would be massive changes in investment strategies thus, logically, there would also be wild changes regarding where money was invested; the economy simply could not, in the short term, withstand this kind of change without enormous hardships for all. A distortion of the reality does a disservice to the individual; clarification of the actual reality to the entire public would adversely affect the individual; you can see the mess that we are in. This again should help reinforce the reason why the public is allowed to live in distortion after distortion. Not every citizen in North America is going to read this book so you can take its advice, using it to your benefit, without the worry of disturbing the present 'balance of unbalance'.

When holding onto money costs you money then the best thing to do is to seek out investments which will alter this situation and if the economic situation comes to the point where all investments become perverse then one should dump all their dollars (paper wealth) for tangible assets. Most people, when they invest, simply look at the gross return on their money but if you want to prosper and actually make money on your money you must also factor in your tax bracket and the present inflation rate, and if you are really advanced, the expected inflation rate for the future.

I believe that one relatively safe investment is **gold.** Gold has always held its value over the long run. Yes, gold does fluctuate up and down over the short-term but if you invest for the long-term you may want to look at gold. Gold has usually kept up with inflation and that cannot be said about too many investments – believe it, it is true! You probably are sceptical again; of course you are. Do you want to know that your investments over the last couple of decades have actually been costing you money – absolutely not! You want to feel that you have made financial progress. If, however, you do not come to understand and deal with the truth, you will continue to invest in investments that are perverse.

Inflation – A Closer Look

Do economists and those in charge of a nation's economic machinery really know what is the true cause of inflation in today's economic climate? I would strongly maintain that they do not. Yes, these are strong words, but inflation is not under control in North America and has not been for quite some time. What really is at the heart of our inflation today is the mountain of debt that corporate sector, government sector, and private sector have accumulated. This is not to say that there are not other factors involved in determining the levels of inflation but debt seems to be playing a key role at this point in time. Lets look at each sector individually to help clarify the issue.

Government Sector

Both the Canadian and American governments spend more than what they take in which leads to a budget deficit. This deficit is funded basically by two methods:

(1) Borrowing
(2) Taxation

Both of these methods have been used to cover the government short-fall in revenue; however, borrowing has become the dominant factor in this scenario. Whether it be through borrowing or taxation, both of these methods lead to inflation. When taxes go up the cost of buying any product or service, which falls under the new tax, goes up in price. This is inflation. When the government borrows money this also leads to inflation, the key reason being that a government having deficits in the billions requires a lot of people to invest in their lending vehicles such as bonds or treasury bills. In order to attract investors to these particular types of investment vehicles, it must attract them away from other investments such as corporate bonds and stocks. They entice investors by the interest rate given on the investment. As interest rates rise, the cost of goods and services goes up. As interest rates rise, the cost of living or doing business for any person or corporation and even the government, for that matter, goes up. As the cost of borrowing goes up revenues and income go down. To offset this decrease in income corporations raise prices, which is inflationary; working people demand more in the way of wages and inflation protection and governments tax and borrow even more.

The Corporate Sector

Many corporations today are saddled with record setting debt loads. Men like Donald Trump and Robert Campeau had companies saddled with enormous amounts of debt; look what has happened to them! It is this type of company that becomes very vulnerable to interest rate hikes. As interest rates move higher, then their debt payments increase dramatically. If they are to stay solvent, they will have to raise more income-generating revenue. If a recession causes revenues to fall, then the cash flow picture becomes only that much more complicated. Raising the levels of revenue can be done in several different ways: (1) Raise prices (2) Sell-off corporate parts, (3) Raise even more capital

Raising Prices

If a company is an industry leader operating as an oligopolist (limited competition exists) or monopolist (competition for all intents and purposes does not exist) then it may get away with large price increases since its competition is limited. If it is in a perfectly competitive situation, meaning that there are many companies competing for the same market, then large price increases may not be in their best interest, or at all feasible, if they wish to retain their particular percentage of market share. However, if the company is a price leader (the company has strong domination in the market place thereby allowing it to basically set prices) then it may increase prices and the rest of the competition will join in. Any price increase whether it be large or small leads to inflation. If the company does not wish to sell off corporate assets or, if there are none left, and the company cannot raise more capital it may be forced to raise prices to its demise however. The rise in prices here may bring temporary relief to a cash crisis but if the competitors do not follow suit, the company may face insolvency due to a shrinking market segment/share. Other companies in the same industry might well not raise prices if their financial statement is not in a precarious situation; they may capitalize on its competitor raising prices and 'steal' away a very important market share.

Raise Even More Capital

The days of raising capital easily are over; the bonanza of the eighties is over, for now. The lucrative junk bond market is no more. It is no wonder that the junk bond market went sour. Many term them high yield bonds rather than junk bonds. *No euphemism has been able to change reality. The junk bond market was just that, junk.* Billions of dollars were raised for many different companies. Often the assets of these companies were grossly overvalued and goodwill was widely enhanced. Raising capital for many companies was a way to avert apparent solvency problems. This is more commonly known as re-financing or re-structuring, again a euphemism that shadows the real words of financial trouble. Everyone on Wall Street and Bay Street was talking and smelling roses when they were actually walking through poison ivy. The distortions of reality were all too clear but have been largely ignored. And let it be dually noted that, still today, many of these realities are being ignored; I will add, caveat emptor – let the buyer beware.

The Public Sector

It was announced in the middle of July, 1990, that Canadians have never in history had the level of debt that they now have. Out society is not a pay-as-you-go society anymore. Most people have large amounts of debt. The pay-as-you-go society is virtually non-existent. This pay-as-you-go society, I would argue, existed up until the middle of the 1900s. The basics of this society were relatively simplistic. In order to buy or trade, one needed either currency or goods to participate in the exchange mechanism.

As interest rates rise, the amount of money needed to service debt also increases. By this I mean that, if your credit cards were at ten percent interest and now they have gone to twelve percent interest, the difference of two percent is going to cost you more money. If you have a lot of debt and interest rates rise your ability to stave off bankruptcy may only be through wage increases. So as wage contracts come due, a main issue will be wages and inflation protection. You will be seeing and hearing much more about these issues. They have also been important but have often lagged behind job security. Job security is going to become less of an issue as interest rates rise in the future.

So back to the original point. It can now be seen that as governments raise interest rates, in order to combat inflation, this actually causes more inflation. This is why the people running the economic machinery such as

Canada's John Crow, Governor of the Bank of Canada, must not really understand inflation if, in fact, their true intention is to reduce it. However, it is rational to assume that in the long-term, inflation will decrease after the economy goes through a major adjustment and correction phase. The problem here is that most likely the economy will have to go into a recession first.

As the economy slows down and heads for recession, unemployment begins to rise. As the unemployment rate rises, workers' demands for higher wages usually decreases as job security becomes more important. No, I am not contradicting myself at this point. As inflation increases, the first demand by workers may well be job security, but if inflation begins to get out of control, job security will become secondary and inflation protection will become the paramount issue.

Is there a Hidden Agenda?

Maybe inflation is not what the government is fighting. It may be that a run on the nation's currency may follow a decrease in the interest rate. The government might have to raise interest rates simply to ensure that there are enough investors, particularly foreign, to finance the government's ongoing budget deficit crisis.

The announcement that government is waging a war on inflation indicates to the public that the government is really concerned with the problem and the effects that will generally have on the well being of the nation's citizens may very well be a way of distorting the real issues of currency stability and government debt levels.

Yes, the budget deficit is definitely a crisis issue. Anyone who tells you otherwise simply does not have a clear picture of North America's financial situation. We are living in a time of false prosperity. If the governments of both Canada and the United States balanced their budgets this fiscal year, there would be a strong possibility that a deep and prolonged depression would strike the countries soon after.

When the economy is growing, the government, in fact, should be balancing its budgets if not running a surplus. The simple logic behind this is that, if the government can not balance a budget in good fiscal/economic times and is expected to run deficits during times of recession, then when will the budget deficits stop?

The reasons why this depression would strike the nations is due to the size of the budget deficits. In Canada this fiscal year, the budget deficit will be approximately thirty (30) billion dollars, and in the United States, it will be approximately one hundred and eighty (180) billion dollars, not including the Savings and Loan mess. If we removed that amount of money from the economy, by forcing the government to balance its budget, we surely would stumble, firstly, into a recession and then, secondly, trip into a depression.

The governments of Canada and the United States are in a precarious position. They require so much money each fiscal year in order to keep from going bankrupt. Some economists will argue that no government can go bankrupt. While this is technically true, realistically any country's government can potentially go bankrupt.

Put simply, a rise in interest rates may be verbally denoted as required to combat inflation but may realistically be required in order to prevent the government from going bankrupt through a constriction in the flow of foreign funds into the country. Let me again explain why interest rates go up when borrowing by government is done. This is a simple point but is often hard to explain. There are many people/countries around the world who invest in our country's treasury bills. We as a country need these investors as our own savings in this country can not cover the budget deficit. If there is another country in the same mess – which there is the United States, for example, also requires investment funds.

It works like an auction with the highest bidder winning. The bids are interest rates paid on investments. We may have to push up interest rates in order to get investors to invest in Canada, rather than in the United States. Since government bonds and treasury bills are fully secured by the full faith of the applicable government, then the only difference between our treasury bill (Canada's) and the United States' treasury bills is the attached interest rate. Thus, both being the same with the exception of interest rate, an investor will choose the one yielding the highest return.

Father

Our Father was pure
His character of helping and aiding was as such
His brilliance illuminated the faces of others
His insides were driven to help cure

The Father began to lust
Seeing and having was just too much
Standing outside he saw a ray
The ray showed him that he need not go bust

The Father, he laughed, played and enjoyed
The unthinkable became the thinkable
He had wealth as never before
He looked in a mirror with a great smile

The Father saw that the day of truth was here
The contents of the glass placed in front of him was
    undrinkable
With nothing else there, he knew he must drink it
Oh, there was so much fear

The Father saw a pure white light slowly consume the
    black ray
Grief and anger consumed his thoughts
Soon sorrow was all there was
This was the beginning of a new day

Our Father saw an old but new direction
It did not matter what was bought
Our Father played and talked with us once again
This was some sort of divine correction

Glenn M.J. Epps

The Joke is on You, Unfortunately

The Paper Money Joke

Paper money was not such a bad idea when it was backed by gold. With it being backed fully by gold it was real money. Today paper money is backed by nothing except faith. *The* United States went off the gold standard in 1971; a fact that *many do not know.*

Gold is real money because it has inherent value. It is a scarce commodity, it doesn't tarnish, it is durable and it is easily refined into various gold products. Paper money not backed by gold is known as a fiat currency. It is money because you believe it is money. Today, different coloured socks could be used as money just as easily as paper money! Again a reality has been created which distorts the traditional reality.

In the past your money was fully backed by the gold reserves of the country. You at any time could exchange your paper money for gold. Today you cannot exchange it for gold and it is backed only by the full faith and credit of the government. In other words, the money you hold in your wallet is backed by a false reality; a corrupt institution is telling you that your money is real and has value.

Paper money today has value because you believe it has value. You can use it to purchase goods and services but this probably will not always be the situation. I believe we are coming to a currency crisis. As debt piles even higher and interest rates stay high relative to the decades after the second world war, government is going to come under continued pressure to start printing money. When the next major recession hits, I believe that government revenues will decrease dramatically; government expenses will skyrocket and corporate America will start to crumble and fall under the heavy weight of debt. This will happen when all the behind-the-scenes activity between government and business to hold the economy together no longer can be pulled off.

The government will have no choice but to print money. The kind of money that they are going to need will not be raised strictly through government auctions and bond sales; billions upon billions are going to be required. It is this kind of scenario that leads to the collapse of a fiat "phony" currency. As dollars roll of the printing presses at faster rates, people will begin to question what is the value behind the dollars that they hold. Foreign investors will also ask the same question. This will lead to a fire sale of dollars. People will want to exchange their worthless paper for tangible assets.

Let's slow down again for a minute and let this become clear to you. I ask you, what gives a dollar value when it is printed? You probably thought gold but we have seen that this is not the case. Can you think of anything else? If you can, please write to me and let me know because I am unaware of anything that gives paper money value, except for faith, in today's world. Take away faith and the dollars you hold and have in the bank revert back to what they truly were all along – just worthless ink and paper. *This is the actual reality – let no man distort this anymore!*.

I strongly believe that we will return to a gold backed currency, not a paper currency but rather a gold backed computer currency. In fact, the Russian's have even proposed such an idea; that is, of a gold backed paper currency. Imagine, the Russian Ruble backed by gold! This would become the currency of the world if no other country followed suit. The American dollar would virtually collapse overnight. You will find that I talk about the potential returns of investing in gold in the investment chapter of this book.

The Bank Joke

I hate to break another one of your learned 'distortions of reality', but I feel that it is always best to be informed rather than uniformed. For every dollar you have on deposit with a chartered bank, the bank only has ten cents in actual cash per deposited dollar. Most of the money that you have on deposit has been lent out to someone else via mortgages, car loans, business loans, to mention just a few. The banks are not a service – they are a business and they are in the business of making money just like any other business operating within the capitalistic structure. The bank pays you, in the form of interest, for the use of your money. This money is then lent out and people are charged for the use of this money again in the form of a borrowing interest rate. On a somewhat simplistic level, the difference between what the bank charges for the use of its money (your money) and the amount they pay you for using your money minus business expenses equals profit.

The bank being a business rather than a service really changes things quite a bit if you think about it. Many cooperative-type institutions are more service-orientated than business-orientated. Often you will own a share in the 'bank' and often you will get money at a cheaper interest rate. A cooperative's mandate is to serve its shareholders which are the depositors. A bank's mandate is also to serve its shareholders which are usually not the depositors. They, of course, are generally the rich and powerful who, with the use of your money, get richer and more powerful. Again, through a careful creative way, the rich and powerful are able to benefit because of the poorer.

The banks do, however, make business mistakes as all businesses do. The only difference is that their mistakes are with your money. The S & L (Savings & Loans) crisis is a good example of this. They made a lot of bad mistakes but did so because of Federal Deposit Insurance and deregulation. This insurance guaranteed that its customers (depositors) would get their money back if the S & L made bad loans and investments. Deregulation increased competition greatly and forced institutions to offer interest rates that truly were exorbitant. It was these two main factors which caused them to become insolvent. It is this kind of thinking by many people, based upon the given business situation, which led to high speculative investments. These did, in fact, prove to be high risk investments, and many became worthless, plunging hundreds of S & L's into liquidity crisis across the United States. Many of these S & L's invested monies into the high yield bond market – you know what I think about that market.

You may say well, who cares? I was covered by the deposit insurance and that is all that matters. I would agree with you if I thought the banking crisis was over but it has, in my opinion, just begun. The S & L's are not the only institutions in trouble. Many large banks are also in trouble. Many have third world loans on their balance sheets but they know they will never collect the principal. In fact, the banks lent more of your money to these countries so that they could pay the interest and not go into default; this kind of business management should have been made illegal – as it was and is immoral. The reality is that the third world countries can not pay off their loans or make full interest payments.

Banks distort this reality by lending them more money so that the actual reality is continually masked. The downside is that this distortion will come to an end eventually. This is an excellent example of a supposed reality which really is a myth. The reality portrayed to the public is that these loans are still good – interest payments are being made. *What a myth.* **These are not loans; they are bad debts and should be treated as such.**

The whole problem here is that, if these loans are written off, they absorb, in many cases, all of the institution's capital. In many cases the value of these loans exceeds the total capital of the bank! The only solution that I see to this problem is to slowly write the loans off. This will absorb bank profits for many years but what other realistic solutions are there?

In the next few years, I see the banking business failing even more, and the sad part is that many people will not get back their deposited monies; in other words, do not count on the banks making decisions that will be beneficial over the long run. Their concern is strictly for the short term as that is what their performance is based upon. The depositors may technically be repaid but it might be with dollars that are worthless due to a runaway inflation. As the government prints money to pay off the depositors, it kicks up inflation which leads to a deterioration in the purchasing power of the dollar.

Earthquakes

Many areas of great economic importance in our world are awaiting the great earthquake. Yes, an earthquake could send the world's economy into a tailspin. These places include Japan, British Columbia, and California. Experts anticipate very large earthquakes in these regions at any time. They may not come tomorrow but they will occur in the future. That is guaranteed by the scientific community. Has man prepared for these inevitable quakes? Only slightly, but what did we expect?

A major earthquake in Japan would have devastating effects, financially, all around the globe. A major earthquake in California would send economic shock waves throughout the United States and even Japan; Japan has considerable land and real estate holdings in the United States. Likewise, a major earthquake in British Columbia, Canada, would have serious effects on the Canadian Economy and would affect pulp and paper and timber prices across the entire globe.

The Secret of Economic Depressions Unveiled

It is the positive net profit margin of a corporation compared with that of an individual which leads to the growth in wealth disparity. The net profit margin is the gross profit margin stated as a percentage minus the percentage increase in workers' wages. If a company does not have a positive net profit margin, it will then fold, thus society, using the capitalistic system, is assured of re-occurring trends of wealth disparity. The system 'weeds' out those companies that do not have a positive net profit margin – only those who do are allowed to operate in the economy. As discussed elsewhere in this book, it is the increase in wealth disparity that sets the economy up for a depression and possible social rebellion and/or revolution. Depressions are caused by economic factors that are built into the capitalistic model. **Without changes to the model, the economy will always be plagued by depressions.**

CHAPTER 5

Preparing for Tomorrow

The wise man is the one that looks to tomorrow.
The fool is the one who thinks of only today
knowing that tomorrow will follow each new day.
The fool may laugh at the wise man today but
will cry some day.

Preparing Yourself

Becoming aware of the truth requires a certain mind-set. Much like an athlete who prepares his body before performing a certain athletic task, the intellect must prepare his mind. You must come to the conclusion that you want to learn the truth. Your mind must be prepared to use your reasoning skills to determine what you believe is correct. You must not want to create a reality – rather you should want to see the reality. Preconceived notions should be put aside; your mind must be open and clean of ingrained thoughts and ideas. What you must understand is that the truth may seem frightening or even depressing but knowing the truth should lift your spirits as you are now one of the informed. You will now be able to make better decisions for you and your family.

When Chaos Hits

Many people may be saying to themselves that the author has outlined a gloomy picture – should I prepare in any other way? This section of the book will make several 'survival' suggestions. These suggestions will not only help you survive but may actually make the up and coming bad years liveable. This section of the book does not cover every 'angle' re survival techniques. If you are interested in more ideas, head to your book store. There are books available on this very subject.

I believe that a near-total economic meltdown is almost unavoidable, with a moderate depression being absolutely unavoidable. Unfortunately, a trend of overspending has continued for too long and is to blame. It would take total world-wide co-operation in order to solve the economic problems that almost every country now faces. Even those countries that seem to be economically sound really are not. This is due to the fact that a majority of countries are not sound. Once the economy of one country collapses, it will indirectly destroy those economies which are seemingly stable.

When this economic collapse comes which is actual reality, you must be prepared. Thousands, even millions, won't be prepared but because you are an enlightened citizen you will be. *You have been able to recognize the 'distortions of reality' uncovering what really exists – you can prepare.* It sounds strange but those who are prepared for the chaos may actually be better off after than before chaos hits as tremendous opportunities will become available; that window of opportunity is beginning to open!

Rechargeable Batteries and Charger

You are likely to experience intermittent power failures and brown-outs. The United States has not been building enough power generating stations, over the last couple of decades to keep up with the power demand of the future. Several energy experts fear that an electrical power shortage is on its way. I also have other fears. When social chaos arrives, it is very likely that groups of rioters, in the big cities will knock-out power all over the city. With batteries and a charger you will be able to use these in a flashlight and/or radio. A radio is important as it will enable you to keep up with news.

Gasoline

Five gallon plastic containers are good. Five to ten gallons of gasoline should be kept for emergency purposes. You never will know when you may be faced with an emergency but do not have enough money for gas. Make sure that you keep relatively fresh gasoline. Three to four months old should be all right.

Portable Cook Stove & Lantern

Many models are available in your nearest camping

supplies store. You do not need the most expensive. All you require is a lantern that will illuminate a room and a stove that will hold a couple of pots in the event of a longer term power failure.

Cans of Hornet Spray/Mace

Make sure that the hornet spray is the type that shoots several feet. This can be carried around with someone, i.e., in a lady's purse and used in the event of an attack. Better than hornet spray would be mace that shoots several feet. Crime is only going to worsen as the economy continues to deteriorate.

Candles

Look around for a real deal! I have found that four for a dollar is a good price. You might find a slightly better deal or you may have to pay a bit more **but buy them.** If the candles are wrapped in plastic, take this plastic off and store the candles in a dry place. This will help dry the candles out, making them burn significantly longer. Again, in the event of a power failure you will have some light.

Shampoo, Soap, Toothpaste & Deodorant

Have extras of these. Make sure you buy them while they are on sale. There may be a point in time when you cannot afford to buy them.

Lightbulbs

Buy low wattage bulbs and keep them stored. When your pocketbook becomes tight, you can switch to lower wattage bulbs in order to save money.

Food

Many books written on the subject of an economic collapse fail to discuss food. I believe the two are mutually inclusive, not exclusive. I am not going to spend a lot of time on this section as my book is devoted more to the subject of the 'distortions of reality'. For a comprehensive look at the subject of food/food storage for bad economic times, I suggest that you pick-up the book by Howard Ruff entitled, "How to Prosper during the Coming Bad Years". A simple suggestion is to buy an assortment of canned and dried goods. Spend at least two hundred dollars per family member; this may well be the best investment in your lifetime! Remember, any amount of money does not satisfy a hungry stomach. **With the canned goods be sure that you rotate.** In other words, if you buy a case of spaghetti sauce containing twenty four cans, then every time you use a can of spaghetti sauce for your every day needs, take it from the box and then replace it with a fresh one purchased from the store. It is important that you continually replace what you use. There could be an overwhelming panic at the grocery stores at any time once the economy collapses, and you do not want to be caught like the rest of the people.

First-Aid Kit

Every household should have a good first-aid kit even if you still do not believe that we are going to face severe economic and social disorder. Items that you should have are: hydrogen peroxide, iodine, scissors, an assortment of bandages, tape, gauze pads, rubbing alcohol, needle, thread, aloe vera gel.

My Thought

It might be noted that many of these survivaL items may not be needed, but it is better to be safe, and prepared, rather than sorry; *I leave no stone unturned.* I prepare myself for what seems to be **realistically** plausible.

The Coming Social Depression

Actually I guess it would be better to say, "The Coming All-Out Social Depression" as we are now in a social recession. I believe that, before the year 2000, we are going to see an uprising of the silent majority in North America. Peoples' lives are chaotic; stress levels are getting out of control and, economically, people are getting further and further into debt even though their salaries are increasing. I believe that there will be an all out tax revolt. This society has been taxed too much, particularly in Canada. In Canada, more of your working time goes to paying taxes than into your own pocket. People do not see the rewards of their hard work because, often, the harder you work, you, in fact, take home less pay relative to previous salaries and tax brackets. The fruits of one's hard work are not being reaped. I contend that this is the factor on which Capitalism rests – hard work will bring a certain level of reward. Eliminate this factor and you have communism.

Our social system/structure is over burdened. People cannot take the pace and lifestyles of today even though we are supposedly more advanced than our predecessors. We are more advanced technologically but not at all advanced socially. Recent actions in California are a good example of the breakdown of social order and conduct. Due to an inability to cope with today's lifestyles, there have been people who have literally taken gun shots at other motorists during traffic jams. This is not an isolated incident; this is a sign of the times. The ability for these people to cope has faltered. You are going to see more and more people unable to cope. Human beings' coping skills have changed only moderately, but the world and society around them has changed and continues to change, dramatically. Today, emotionally speaking, humans are essentially the same as they were hundreds of years ago. People are still greedy, still jealous, still envious, still competitive, still vulnerable to rejection and change. Notably however, we as humans have changed dramatically socially, economically and technically.

There are even more frightening signs of the coming social depression. Today, schizophrenia is on the increase and so is depression; these are two major mental disorders. In fact, previous statistics on depression indicate that the average age for a person falling into a depression state was the mid-forties. It is now the mid-thirties. We are also seeing a great increase in child and teen depression. I contend that it is an inability to cope with today's peer pressures, financial pressures, career pressures and the breakdown of the basic family unit which is causing these changes. An all-out social depression can only be averted if society looks critically at itself today and makes the necessary changes required for achieving success, particularly emotionally. Mental disorders can change the most productive person into a non-productive person who becomes dependent upon others in order to achieve the simplest of tasks. Further, every member of this society needs to become self-scrutinizing and make changes from the heart and mind, even if others are not. If one does this, you will increase your chances and your children's chances at achieving overall success. As talked about previously, today's ways are not the way to all-encompassing success.

Look at how we as a society treat serious issues. In my opinion, a perfect example involves AIDS and the vast array of other sexually-transmitted diseases. Over the past few decades people have become more and more promiscuous. To most, this has come to be known as the sexual revolution. Face it, promiscuity does not lead to permanent happiness, rather it satisfies temporary physical needs. As promiscuity rose so did the chances of getting one of the many different sexually-transmitted diseases. The number of diseases being transmitted also increased yet there still was a continued rise in promiscuity. In fact, sleeping around today could literally kill you by way of AIDS. What do we do as a society? We do not emphasize monogamy for adults and abstinence for our youth. Instead, we emphasize the use of condoms which helps reduce the risk.

The realities of today lead to discontentment and unhappiness and, in many cases, even death. Unfortunately, mankind seems to repeat itself – it repeats mistakes.

Many empires have risen and fallen. At the heart of every collapse seems to be a breakdown in the social system/structure. Societies have been founded on the assertion of strong morals and values. As time passes, the founding members of the society pass away and so do the original founding ideologies. The society soon finds itself living in a different world than those of our great ancestors. We now live in a time that is much different than what our great ancestors would have imagined. Their age-old principles have, over the decades, been slowly replaced with more modern principles; these modern principles really are out-of-date as they just do not work.

Suggestions have been made throughout the book in order that you may prepare yourself for the continuation of the breakdown of our society.

CHAPTER 6

Investments

A State of Deterioration

Today, we see many people who have been retired for many years but are broke. They are barely able to satisfy basic human needs. When they retired, they were quite comfortable but today they can not make ends meet. They have gone through a state of deterioration. There is probably someone in this situation that you know of. Many of these people blame themselves but they should not. They may think that they made poor investments or spent too much money. The fact is that they probably made poor investments but through no fault of their own.

The government has been starving for money. Therefore, they want us and have actively been encouraging us to buy their financial investments such as Canada Savings Bonds or US/Canadian government Treasury Bills. The government borrows from society's people in order to cover budget deficits and the cost of maintaining these deficits.

The government does not dare tell society that these investments are poor at best and actually cost you money at worst. The 1989 and 1990 series Canada Savings Bonds offered lower rates of interest than compared with a GIC/CD (Guaranteed Investment Certificate/Certificate of Deposit) – a simple investment tool which could be purchased at any bank. This may not be the best investment either but, for those who must stick with conventional investments, the logical choice seems to be the GIC/CD rather than the government instrument.

Investment firms do not tell you either. They make their money by way of your investing money with or through them. Most investment firms offer traditional investments such as stocks and bonds but these traditional investments are exactly that – traditional. The economy has grown much more complex over the last fifty years yet many investment advisors offer and suggest only traditional investments. The economy has become super dynamic and so should one's investments. Sure and safe is going to lead to sorry and sad tomorrow!

How many people can remember their financial advisor giving real rates of return on monies invested? Probably not too many, if any at all. Here is the irony – a great many investors do not know what they are doing! If they did we would not have a majority of this society's people investing in poor rate of return investments and perverse investments. Many seniors are broke today but supposedly invested their money wisely through a knowledgeable investment advisor.

The next time you are at a bank, ask one of the staff what the real rate of return on their GIC/CD is. Or, for that matter, ask your supposedly knowledgeable investment advisor. They probably will not know what you are talking about or will be unable to furnish you with the information. If the board says eleven and three quarters percent, they will say the rate of return is eleven and three quarters percent. **The investment advisor will try very nicely to move on to another topic.**

You, as an informed individual, realize that this is not the true rate of return on an investment. Many investment people have advised people to invest in such instruments. Many bankers tell clients what an excellent rate of return they are getting but one must realize that these people are biased. This seems so obvious but many people miss this point altogether. The banker wants your money because the more he gets, the more the bank makes and the more the bank makes, the more he will make. Most people probably believe that their bankers know a lot about investing – some do but many more do not. Shop around and find a banker that you like and one who talks sensibly to you; this may take a while but keep searching. I have mentioned this point earlier but I believe that its importance warrants emphasizing it once again.

To prosper in this society, one has to be as dynamic as the society and economy is. By this, I mean you must be willing to change your views of investing as political, social, and economic conditions change. The economy is much more dynamic today than what it used to be. Years ago, one would buy a house and would have a fixed mortgage rate until that house was paid for. They could be fairly certain with only small wage increases, very low inflation and they could count on low levels of unemployment. Today, everything is different. Things change by the day and even by the hour. Everything changes and you must, as well. *Conventional* investments in an unconventional world just do not work.

Gold as an Investment

I believe that the price of gold is going to go through the roof. As the economy starts to crumble the demand for gold will increase drastically. **Gold will transport any money you have from point A to point B** – point A being before the financial meltdown to point B which will be the new social and economic order.

I also believe that we will see a gold-based currency again. As mentioned earlier, this will not be a paper currency but rather a currency on computers. The devastation financially will be so great that no one will trust a fiat currency which is only backed by trust and faith. Gold at its present value of approximately four hundred US dollars will not be high enough in order to back a new world currency. I, therefore, conclude that the price of gold will have to be revamped. This could mean that gold may someday be worth thousands of dollars an ounce.

The Dos and Don'ts of Gold

Point (1)
If you purchase gold try to remain an anonymous owner of this gold. If you are required to give a name at the time of purchase, make one up. Try to purchase gold from places that ask very few questions; for your sake, the fewer the better.

Point (2)
Do not tell anyone that you own gold. Gold will become worth so much and, if someone knows you own it, you

could be putting yourself in a dangerous position. Even close family members should be kept in the dark; people do crazy things when money is involved.

Point (3)
Do not keep your gold in a safety deposit box. I believe the government will initially confiscate gold – they have done it before. I believe that the government will pass legislation requiring the banks to open up your safety deposit box in front of you and confiscate any gold contained therein. Instead of keeping it at the bank, buy a small fire proof box and store it somewhere safe in your house. You may even want to bury it in your yard late at night.

Point (4)
Make sure you buy bullion and not gold certificates. The confiscation of gold certificates is relatively simple but more complex for bullion. It is better to be over cautious rather than not cautious enough and get caught losing your precious investment.

How much gold should you have? This is ultimately up to you but I have a general suggestion. My belief is that for every thousand dollars of debt and/or one thousand dollars worth of net assets, you should have one hundred dollars in gold. A 1:10 ratio. I believe that between the rise in gold prices plus the drop in overall prices, this ratio will allow you to retain most of your pre-crash net worth. If your net worth is negative, your gold holdings will allow you to pay off your debts requiring perhaps only one tenth of the money.

If you feel uncomfortable with this ration of 1:10 then you should adjust it to a ratio that you feel comfortable with such as 1:6 or maybe you feel that 1:10 is too high. You may want a ratio of 1:16. Ultimately, you will have to make the decision of whether you even want to purchase gold bullion and, if so, how much. My suggestions are simply that – suggestions.

Gold Stocks

The value of gold stocks will also see great appreciation in the future. As the demand and price of gold skyrockets, so will the price of gold stocks. Before purchasing any gold stocks please check into the company to make sure that it is reputable. Long established Canadian Gold Mining Stocks should be good investments.

Other Stocks

In my opinion, most stocks will be bad investments. I do, however, recommend those stocks that have corporate operations that relate to gold mining, bankruptcy, consulting, accounting, environment protection and high-tech super computer systems.

Bankruptcies will be out of this world and will have to be dealt with. Many balance sheets will need major adjustments and the environment will be a greater concern in the future. The new world order will have a large demand for super computers, especially with the implementation of a cashless society. This is the impetus for these types of suggested stock investments.

Silver

I believe that silver will have good gains but in general will not keep up with the increase in gold prices. Silver is a good investment if you cannot afford gold bullion. Again, demand bullion, not silver certificates, and try to buy anonymously. Basically follow the same rules with silver as with gold.

Certificates of Deposits/Bonds

I believe that, generally, these will be bad investments; they are already poor investments. Even if they are backed by the federal government, the money you are given may be worthless, which we talked about in the inflation section. These are conventional investments that will not afford you the returns given that the economic environment of the future will be most unconventional. My general investment theory for the upcoming depression is that it's better to be safe than broke, so buy gold.

Personal/Consumer Loans

If you have a personal loan, try to lock in the interest rate. You may see a temporary decrease in interest rates but I only see that there will be inevitable increase in interest rates. If you have high outstanding balances on credit cards try to get a personal consolidation loan, at a locked-in rate, from your banker. Even if you do not believe that a depression is on its way, this will still make good sense. Many credit card interest rates are almost double the rate of a fixed rate loan. The reason why you want to lock in rates is rational if you believe that interest rates may rise. Be careful not to look only at the short-term. I do believe that they may fall in the short-term but as the world's economy and social order collapse, interest rates will rise.

CHAPTER 7

The Coming Dawn

Man's devices of destruction must never be used today or any other day. Surely the sun will rise day after day as long as man obeys. With each new day comes many new challenges but with the truth uncovered, tomorrow shall surely be better than today.

An Expert?

Today, most people are turning to so-called experts to help them sort out the confusion of today's world in order that they might be able to get a glimpse at tomorrow's world. The reality is that most experts are not experts about the future. They do not have a sound knowledge about the true realities of this world needed to make educated guesses about what tomorrow will look like. In fact, many experts actually add to the distortions in our society.

Unfortunately, today, our society requires an expert to be legitimized, usually via higher education and the receipt of a degree. This is a shame because many people are very intelligent and very knowledgeable but are unable to contribute their wealth of knowledge to our societal system. Many companies have only helped entrench this into the system. They have done this by requiring certain educational standards for the various jobs that they offer. I can recognize that, in order to do certain jobs, a great deal of formal post-secondary education is required but, on the other hand, many jobs do not require post-secondary education. It is these jobs that should be granted to people on the *basis of ability* and not achieved academic success. I have been asked, "how do we determine ability?". Ability is determined by looking at a person's track record, quizzing the person on issues relevant to the job and also assessing whether the person can do the job or not. It should be recognized that there is a great difference between 'basis of ability' and 'achieved academic success'. To discriminate against a person who does not have a formal degree but who, in fact, does have the necessary abilities and motivation instead hiring the person who has the degree but not necessarily the abilities required, is truly a mistake of stupidity. The 'intelligent' employer will clearly recognize the benefits of both and certainly realize the limitations of hiring based solely upon the 'required need' for a post-secondary degree.

Knowledge, in many cases, does not come from books and learning at school; rather, it comes from living and working every day and gaining a sense of the variables that exist. This is referred to as practical knowledge. Many writers of theoretical books and texts simply do not have the ability to intellectually create and understand a *working model* of the social/economic/environmental package. They generally are able to understand a particular area, describing it in quite some detail, but lack the ability to combine several variables all at once – this is a reality. Functional knowledge comes through practical experience rather than theoretical books and texts.

What do I see for the future?

Seeing accurately into the future requires a person who has gained a knowledge of the truth. A crystal ball is not needed. Learning what is true and untrue, uncovering the 'distortions of reality', leads to a perceptual power that most people do not have. By perceptual power, I mean a person who has the ability to perceive the true long-term trends. Short-term predictions I believe are very hard to make. The world is so dynamic that it is next to impossible to determine what will happen tomorrow. Did anyone expect the invasion of Kuwait by Iraq, the Chernobyl disaster, or the Exxon Valdez disaster?

Long term predictions can be equally as hard to determine if you do not have some sort of perceptual power. One must be able to determine what sources of information are based in truth and which ones are based upon 'distortions of reality'. Once one has gained a clear picture of the true information, then one can put all the pieces together and predict a future event based upon determining a correct or next to correct long term trend.

This sounds confusing doesn't it? Well it certainly can be. Like anything, it takes practice and most of all a willingness to see through issues, getting to the true heart of the matter. If you live in distortion after distortion of reality you will never be able to determine a correct long-term trend. Knowledge of 'actual reality' is paramount in order to do realistic long-term forecasting. Let me walk you through an example of this forecasting method which I will call E.F.M.; the **Epps Forecasting Method.**

Forecast:

I believe that the debt of the countries around the world will never be repaid and that most of it will eventually have to be written off. These would include the debts of countries from both the first and third worlds such as the United States, Canada, Mexico, Brazil and Latin America.

Sources:

POINT 1. Many economists will tell you that there is nothing to worry about. These debts will have no major impact upon the economy.

POINT 2. Countries such as the United States and Canada now borrow just to pay the interest on the federal debt.

POINT 3. We have just come through the biggest economic growth period since the end of World War II yet we have seen an historic increase in debt.

POINT 4. Countries such as Brazil and Mexico are struggling to survive under the pressure of crushing debt loads. The people of these countries are already today facing untold economic hardship because of these debt burdens.

POINT 5. Ronald Reagan and George Bush have reassured the public that the fundamentals of the economy are sound.

POINT 6. As our population ages, there will be even more need for funds. The debt burden will soar.

Analysis of Points:

POINT 1: Economists present an image of soundness, and knowledge. Many economists do not know what they are talking about – this is simple reality. Many economists say that everything in the economy is virtually fine. What are they going to tell you, take your money and run?

POINT 2: This is a true fact, this is reality!

POINT 3: If the past seven to eight years have been good, I must then assume that, under bad economic conditions, which we always have at some point in time, debt burdens will absolutely soar. They soared in good times; actual reality dictates that they will soar even further during bad times.

POINT 4: I believe that through political extreme pressures right now, countries such as Mexico and Brazil are paying on their debts. It is also reality that these countries are having to borrow in order to pay interest payments. I do not believe that the leaders of these countries will sink with the ship. There will be a last-ditch effort, economically speaking, to survive when the world economy worsens. It is at this point that it would become realistic to expect that these countries will suspend all debt and interest payments.

POINT 5: One must question what is the reality surrounding national leaders such as Bush and Reagan. This is very simplistic but evades most. *The job of an elected* politician is to either get himself re-elected or someone else from his own party elected. Knowing this, one can expect that national leaders will distort many issues in order to slant them in their favour. At a time when many people questioned the soundness of the economy, particularly after the stock market crash, both Reagan and Bush said it was absolutely solid. In fact, Reagan said he did not understand why the crash happened. You do not have over a five hundred point drop in one day for no reason! I must ask you why they had to reassure the public that the economy was sound? Who do you believe – the truly concerned citizens, economists and business people or the national leaders who have an agenda that requires them to try and get re-elected?

POINT 6: The reality is that the demographics are changing in this society. Our population is aging. With that comes a great need for financial resources. Money is going to be required for retirement homes, hospital care, nursing homes, medication, special devices and much more. In other countries the birth rate is relatively high and this condition will require money for food, drugs, immunization, education and clothing. If we do not have money for these now, where will it come from in the future? There is not a magical wand that can be waved to stop these problems from haunting our society.

Conclusions

The sources of information which are based in reality seem to clearly indicate that there will be a growing need for money! The long-term trend is fairly clear. Debt will continue to increase until we reach the point where we can no longer pay it, just as the third world countries are experiencing.

Forecast from the Conclusions

We will reach a time in the future when the governments of the Western countries will default on their debt. Technically a government cannot default as it has the ability to print money but my belief is that, if the governments pay back a creditor in worthless dollars this is synonymous with default. This will have absolutely devastating effects all over the world and, in all likelihood, every individual on this planet will be affected.

Using the E.F.M., I will make some additional forecasts without going through the details of how I arrived at them; but, believe me, it was not done overnight and it was not with a tea cup and tea leaves. I am not like the astrological Reagans, who ran the United States based upon 'tea leaf' predictions; another word for predictions is uneducated guesses. God help America if Bush follows the same methods as his former boss!

All of the following forecasts were made during the summer months of 1990, unless otherwise stipulated.

The Family

I believe there will be a general return to the traditional family unit. After great experimentation, the results show that a strong family unit, consisting of natural parents is a far superior institution than that of the "step" family. The breakdown of the family unit is today's worst social disaster. It has caused countless hardships both emotionally and financially.

World Powers:

The United States

I believe that the United States will fall from its present position of world leader. Its large arsenal of nuclear weapons will always reserve it a place at world events and meetings. World leader status will not be respected after the world sees the United States' inability to pay back its debts, causing untold hardship for billions around the globe.

The European Community

I think we are going to see the European Economic Community (EEC) come to be the new world leader/power.

There will be bickering back and forth between leaders over the issue of political autonomy, but these will be resolved. This main issue will be resolved by a powerful charismatic leader.

The present twelve countries that form the European Economic Community will not be the final countries making up the European Power. Surprisingly enough I believe that the world will see some of the Eastern Bloc countries comprising the European Power. This will be able to be realized due to the world recognizing the full autonomy of these countries. Power/boarder shuffling will take place in the future. To include some of the Eastern Bloc countries in the new European Super Power will have great political advantage.

This European Community leader will not be someone from the typical political background. Not coming from an extremely political background will help better legitimize his position and intentions as there will be no specific overt/covert political agendas; he will be the first in a era of new political leaders. I see this leader being someone relatively young, somewhere in his early forties. This young spirited person will help energize Europe. Broken apart, the individual countries are not very significant, but put together they become an awesome force to be reckoned with.

Japan

I do not believe that Japan will be a major force in the future. I do believe that it will continue to be a leader technologically. Japan is in a temporary position of influence. Its privileged financial status makes it what it is today. This status will change when we come to the next depression. Billions of Yen will be wiped out. Many great fortunes will be lost. The Japanese will lose billions of dollars of overseas investments such as that of US Treasury Bills. The United States will never be able to repay Japan what it has borrowed. Japan will be paid off in worthless dollars.

Since Japan has no natural resources of its own, it only stands to reason that it cannot continue to be a world leader. I say this because Japan must import all its raw materials; this costs money. It may have the technology but not the resources. The countries with the resources, given the technology, would stand to become more efficient at producing the goods than Japan would. Given time, the countries presently lacking the technologies but who have the resources will obtain the needed technology. These countries then will be naturally pre-disposed to have an economic advantage re the production of goods. No country retains power over the long run without having substantial natural resources.

I see Japan as having a middle-man type role. Without artificial barriers to trade such as duties and tariffs, the laws of economics dictate that the long run trend will be a trend towards the greatest efficiency. Japan has been able to distort the true long-term reality with its own short-term reality. This short-term reality is, in fact, a distortion of the actual reality. Through its aggressive nature to become technologically more advanced than many other industrial-ized countries, Japan has been afforded a temporary position of world leader, economically speaking. We are going to see "The Setting of the Sun in the Land of the Rising Sun". See the diagram entitled, "The Trading Model" on the next page.

The Trading Model

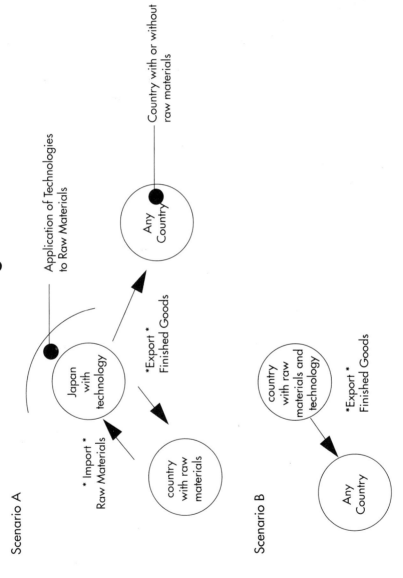

Scenario A

Application of Technologies to Raw Materials

Country with or without raw materials

Any Country

*Export * Finished Goods

Japan with technology

* Import * Raw Materials

country with raw materials

Scenario B

country with raw materials and technology

*Export * Finished Goods

Any Country

"The Trading Model", depicts two different scenarios, Scenario A and Scenario B. Scenario A shows Japan's role in the trading model. Japan has technology but must import raw material from any country having these raw materials. Japan then applies its technology to these raw materials creating a finished good ready for export. These finished goods will be exported to any country demanding the product including the country that sold Japan the raw materials in order to manufacture the finished product.

Scenario B is the most efficient scenario. It has cut out the middle man, Japan. Any reductions in middlemen decrease production costs and therefore decrease the purchase cost of a product thereby enhancing overall efficiency and decreasing inflationary tendencies. The country with the raw material has gained the technology needed to produce the finished good. It produces the goods (widgets) from start to finish, exporting the finished goods to countries having appropriate demand.

Russia

I have left in my forecast for Russia as it was written untouched.

Forecast, written in August 1990

I do not believe that Mikhail Gorbachev will be able to hold onto power. In fact, there is a real possibility that he may be assassinated. His present political agenda is very threatening to many politically powerful leaders within his own country. Up until this point staunch communists have allowed Gorbachev to try and straighten Russia's dismal economic position. Even if Gorbachev makes progress, he is doing it at the expense of the order of communism. To get the economic engine going, he is mixing "Communist" fuel with "Western" fuel. This gives rise to the potential of having communism replaced with a new form of governing rule. Rebellion is already taking place in the satellite countries and there is the potential that it may spread to the heartlands of Russia.

I am a great believer in the repetition of history. I cannot see that communism will 'peter out' without the staunch hard liners trying to take the position of authority and power again. Very few political regimes have come and gone without a fierce fight. The 'to the death' fight has yet to start in Russia's political gallery.

New Forecast for Russia – Given that the expected change occurred

Forecast, August 1991.

I still do not see Mikhail Gorbachev holding onto power over the long run. Even though he has returned to power, his power base has weakened even further. The communist doctrine will not be lost overnight. Also, the people of Russia have had a taste of Western Democracy and to them it seems great. What they have yet to experience is a Western-created worldwide depression. Yes, Russia is in a severe economic position right now but a distortion of reality exists in the minds of the Russian people. They believe that the Western democratic capitalist system will bring them out of their present mess. The reality is that Mikhail Gorbachev is leading them from one economic slaughter house to another economic slaughter house. Changes are coming at a very bad time as the impending worldwide depression will make the Russian people leery of the Western political/economic setup.

A very dangerous situation is being created in Russia at this very moment. Momentum and enthusiasm for any kind of change is snowballing in Russia. There will be a strong effort in the future to unite Russia and establish itself as the world power! It seems clear to me that Russia and the now independent satellite countries will have to maintain some kind of unity – particularly economic.

China

China has a strange 'mix'. On one hand it is a relatively poor country yet on the other hand it has been a member of the nuclear arms club for quite some time. This leads me to believe that there is an agenda that the Chinese have – an agenda that will shock and surprise the world. I predict that this poor country will try to grab hold of world power. Their army size combined with their nuclear weapons makes them a formidable force.

Its poorness is allowing it to pursue its desire for world power unnoticed. A thorough investigation of Chinese military capabilities should be done immediately. Any country having a nuclear arsenal should be closely monitored.

The world got a quick glance at Chinese policy during the Tieanamen Square massacre, yet its wide scope implications and meanings went unnoticed. It is a policy that has no regard for human life – a policy that is faithful to the Communist Chinese Party.

Whoops, I almost forgot the Middle East

The Middle East (January 1992)

Tensions, tensions, tensions...the Middle East is a terribly volatile area of the world. This area is unstable because of political agendas, religious agendas, land area agendas, personal agendas, hidden agendas and overt agendas. These are only some of the factors involved. This middle east model is so complicated that nobody truly understands it. Thus, we see an inability to introduce successful lasting negotiated settlements to long standing issues. Some people like to think that a peaceful solution to the multitude of problems that exist is just around the corner. Unfortunately, it is not. In fact, as the world economic system continues to decline, things will only get worse. Poor economic times negatively affect any of major negotiations and peace proposals.

If anyone thinks that Israel is going to concede some of its territory to the Palestine Liberation Organization (PLO) or any groups of people, then you should think again. 1948 was a climatic event for all the Jewish people around the world as it marked the establishment of their country. The significance of this event is underestimated by many today. The major political leaders of today, who are proposing that a peaceful settlement is more than likely going to have to include Israel giving up some of its territory, are simple dreaming. I believe that the Americans, will see this as a basic requirement for the peace process to continue. Because of this, I anticipate that a rift will come between the American and Israeli governments. With this position, Israel will stand on its own in the world community. Israel will certainly be looking for support and assistance in solving its problems. The direction that they look may well be to that of the emerging European Super State.

The Jews, for thousands of years, have been persecuted and without a common home. Jewish people are scattered from one corner of the earth to the other. The small state of Israel helps foster the bonding of Jewish people all over the world. Whether Jews live in the United States, Canada, Russia, or Australia they commonly have a homeland to which they can refer - Israel. It is much like when a young child gets lost in a large shopping mall. Once reunited, the child holds on tight to the parents hand so that he will not get lost again. The Jewish people where lost and are now reunited; a Jew was that child and is not going to let go of their country.

I believe that the peace process concerning the above issues will get worse before it gets better. As I said, as the economic state of the world continues to deteriorate this will add complexity to an already immensely complex problem.

The rich oil Gulf States are going to be in for a shock in the near future. The situation that exists here is somewhat similar to that in Japan. The Gulf States have billions of dollars invested in American securities, real estate and so forth. Most of these off-shore investments will be lost. The will cause a short-term economic crisis. Also, as the world community tumbles into a deep depression, the demand for oil will drop putting tremendous downward pressure on the price of oil. At that point, fighting amongst the Organization of Petroleum Exporting Countries (OPEC) members may cause the organization to break down completely. Yes, we well may see the end of OPEC in the not to distant future.

The Gulf States will not endure long-term economic hardship. When the world comes out of the depression, demand for various products and services will be extremely large. Growth rates of the economies of the various countries around the world will be incredible. Economic growth rates will top the best figures that ever have been recorded. This will lead to an enormous demand for oil. This will reverse the downward pressure on the price of oil causing the price to rise. Fantastic investment opportunities will be able to be realized at this time. The key will be to invest when oil prices turn around for a longer term upswing. Be wary of normal fluctuation in oil prices. A move at the wrong time could cost you a great deal of money. Before you invest be sure that you are aware of actual reality.

A New World Order

A time of catastrophic economic conditions always opens up the issue of world order for discussion and/or change. The World Order includes who is regarded as being the lead economic/political power. It also includes the type of political/economic set up that exists. We in the West have what is called Western Democracy. It varies from country to country but, essentially, all countries have democracy and a capitalistic type system.

I strongly believe that a New World Order is on its way. I believe that the European Economic Community will head it. I also believe that we will see a different form of Western

Democracy. Forecasting what it will be is very difficult. All that I really am certain about is that capitalism will not exist as we presently know it.

A New World Order will be the result of reshuffling of world powers. It will also be the strengthening of the United Nations' concept to help combat worldwide problems. So many problems now face this world that a new order is needed to deal with them. Essentially, we will see a world-wide government. Individual countries around the world will still retain much of their autonomy but much will also be removed.

I see the strong possibility of a World Order that has both the benefits of communism mixed with the benefits of capitalism. This kind of new mix, I believe, would generate terrific wealth and would see world problems being dealt with.

Trends

Trends may take years to become recognizable as a trend. Today, we are seeing a mass convergence of many longer-term trends. You can perceive this as an eclipse. Only every so often are the moon, the sun and the earth in positions that will produce a total eclipse. Short-term changes in the positions of the earth, moon, and sun lead to the long-term an eclipse.

We are now facing a period in history where we will be living with the very poor decisions of the past; the selfish decisions of the past. The convergence of the trends are economic, political, social and environmental. I personally do not believe that, in the entire history of man, all these trends have converged at the same time with all of the attached problems.

It certainly is not my intention to depress or sadden anyone but the truth needs to be heard. It is my belief, as I have reiterated time and time again, that one cannot deal with unknowns. It is only when the truth (reality) is revealed to the individual and/or public that any realistic actions can be taken.

If present trends continue into the future, without change, I believe that the existence of the human race, as we have come to know it, will come into jeopardy. I am not saying that the race will cease to exist but I believe the ability of the earth to sustain current world populations will not endure.

Trends can, in fact, be broken but it seems that mankind does not act on any issue unless it presents itself as a serious problem already adversely affecting much of the population. The inhabitants of this earth cannot wait this long. The past was unique in that man did not know the way to do massive destruction to his environment.

Short-Term Trends

As said several times throughout the book, short-term trends may be seemingly insignificant but it is the short-term trends that lead to the long-term trends. Long-term trends are significant and careful attention should be paid to them.

As can be seen by the diagram, "Trends", on the next page there are many short-term trends with various intensities but next to none are converging. The non-convergence of trends is what produces complacency in man. When trends do not converge, the world and its problems seem workable and, no major crisis appears, thereby legitimizing many of the current decisions and/or policies. Some short-term trends do intersect, but many do not. It is this process that produces gradual change as opposed to various forms of radical change, generally seen as a crisis.

Trends

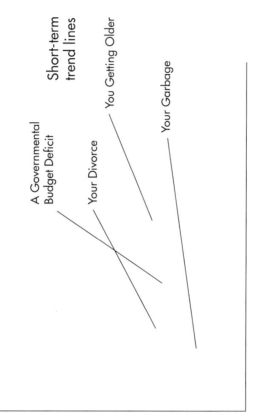

Intensity of trends

A Governmental Budget Deficit

Your Divorce

Short-term trend lines

You Getting Older

Your Garbage

Time

Long Term Trends

Long term trends are created, nurtured, or eliminated through short-term trends. For example, short-term trends of scientists researching for a substance that could be used as a coolant created CFC's. Short-term trends of endorsement and use of CFC's nurtured the now growing long-term trend of destruction to the ozone layer in the upper atmosphere. This long-term trend may come to an end through various short-term trends which would be the creation of laws that stop the production of CFC's. It is critical that we identify both short and long-term trends in order that the elimination of longer term trends – which are negative – can happen as soon as possible.

Long-term trends tend to converge at some point. This time of conversion is what I call the focal point. This focal point has an attached characteristic which is either, positive (+10), neutral (0), negative (-10), or somewhere in between.

Today, there are a multitude of longer-term trends converging which will result in a complete convergence in the near future. Unfortunately, the reality is that the focal point is a strong negative (-8); (-10) would represent a worldwide nuclear holocaust.

See the next page for the diagram "Convergence of Trends".

Convergence of Trends

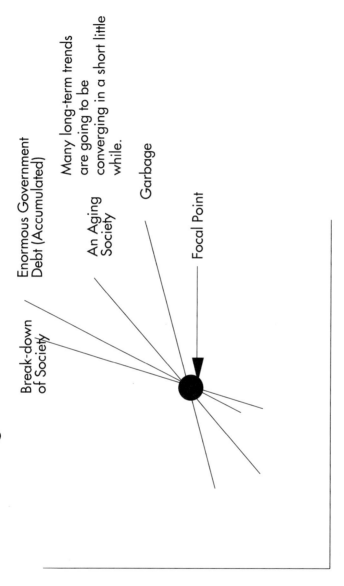

Break-down of Society

Enormous Government Debt (Accumulated)

An Aging Society

Garbage

Many long-term trends are going to be converging in a short little while.

Focal Point

Time

Specific Trends

There are two ways of looking at these converging trends. One is pessimistic while the other is optimistic and/or realistic in this particular case.

The pessimistic view is one that sees only pain and suffering for themselves and others. They see only a dark cloud descending onto this earth – a dark cloud that will bring misery and headache to countless people. The realistic view, which in this case I believe is synoptic with the optimistic view, is much different. The nonconvergence of many of these long-term trends has produced complacency in man. Inaction is the way to describe the last few decades. The convergence of trends is going to shake the whole world community. It is going to have a positive effect on man and his actions. Inaction will no longer be tolerated. I believe those people who want to do something for their country and fellow man will replace those politicians that are mainly there for the 'gravy'.

A worldwide think tank will probably be created which will dwarf any similar organization to this date. Many issues including life-threatening environmental issues will be dealt with and not in a superficial way. The need for the world community to work together will promote worldwide peace. It will be at this time when the world will see the creation of the world's first effective world-governing body. Political will, policy and power is presently fragmented around the entire world. This conflicts with man's growth. Today there is a much greater need to have a world political apparatus than there was one hundred years ago.

Because of worldwide links through the economy and the environment, a pressure is being created for some form of centralized power structure. I believe that it will be a greatly enhanced version of our United Nations organization of today.

Trying to change the present trends will require a **massive** amount of individual action. Citizens can no longer afford to be passive – they must become interactive. Write to your local political representative. *Explain to him that you want some definite action taken on the environment and economic situation and not just token gestures.* Indicate that you know the real truth – that both the economy and environment are in dire need of repair. Indicate that you will only support someone who has an interest in both the long and short-term trends. Each individual taking this kind of step will be initiating a change to the destructive trends which now exist in this world.

If you do not want to take this kind of step for yourself, then do it for your children, and the children of this world as they will be inheriting the future world. Please note that there are a couple of letters in the back that you may want to send to your political representative. All that is left up to you is the determination of a name and address. You are free to use these letters as is.

Canada and the United States at the Crossroads

Both of these two great countries are at crossroads. One of these roads leads to success while the other leads to a road which will take these two countries down a continuous decline. Both these countries have deficits that get bigger and bigger each day and, also, they both have terrible social problems such as drugs, crime and the breakdown of the family unit. Does this have to be the way? I do not think so. There are alternatives that would bring renewed prosperity to both these countries.

These countries must both rebuild their foundations. The foundation of morals and values has greatly crumbled. Without decent morals and values, there can be no ad infinitum success. Slowly, as the moral/value foundation crumbles, so does the country. The family unit, work ethics, respect for law and order, respect for individuals – just to name a few – have all deteriorated. This is happening across the board within these two countries. Not one person is able to escape the effects or side-effects of these problems. As these problems grow so does the infrastructure needed to deal with them. By infrastructure I mean hospitals, drug treatment programs and correctional institutions.

The emphasis, for economic reasons, needs to shift from hopeless efforts directed at symptom management to efforts directed at the root cause. There needs to be a major allocation of new funds to an all-encompassing health care program, education, housing, and crime prevention. Why a shift must take place is because there are realistically only so many dollars to go around. With the onset of social problems comes the need to deal with them, which of course, has an attached financial cost. In order for North America to survive and prosper economically and socially the priorities re allocation of tax dollars must be dealt with.

North America with its natural resources far exceeds any country or groups of countries on this planet for potential of being successful. The right combination between labour (human input) and technology could produce amazing productivity gains and profits right into the new millennium. Our countries have at their finger tips the ability to be super-dynamic. One must remember however that these kinds of PERMANENT gains can only be made over the long-term. No short-term miracle exists that is going to lead to long term improvements.

That is a major problem of today – the focus is on the short term. The Reagan miracle really was not a miracle as such. Reagan did get the economic wheels moving again but not in a fashion that would see them move continuously into the future. The miracle was based "solely" on a short-term cure. What he did was borrow great amounts of money from various investors all over the world and then threw it into the economy. As Lloyd Benson of the Democratic party stated, the economic Reagan miracle was based upon a series of hot cheques. The economic wheels turn when money is spent in the economy. When Reagan came into office, the economic wheels were turning slowly, so in order to get them moving faster, Reagan borrowed from abroad so he could spend billions of dollars in the United States. Much of the spending was in the way of an enormous military build up.

This kind of allocation of resources is very inefficient. Money is spent on military apparatus. Sure, there are a few spinoffs for the rest of the economy but, basically, the money goes into research and development that will directly effect the military. Great amounts of money are spent on a "military machine" that will only age, giving little back to the economy in the long run. What this spending spree on the military did achieve was to get the Republicans re-elected which is a short-term orientation. They really did not have you in mind when they were spending – **they had themselves in mind.**

For the United States and Canada to prosper, a long-term outlook will be required just as the Japanese have; their current empire was not built in a few years. The United States and Canada could have similar success, actually better success – all that is needed are good decisions, time and nurturing.

Short-term gains, long-term pains.
Short-term pains, long-term gains.

Centralized Power the Route to Dictatorship

History has shown us time and time again that central-ized power often leads to the abuse of that power – essentially dictatorship. There are many examples: Napoleon, Caesar and Hitler to name just a few. There may be good reasons for centralized power but there are just as many, if not more, reasons not to have centralized power.

Using history as a teacher, which would be a new concept for man, it seems that some man will find a way to corrupt power structures, especially those which embody "pure" power. By pure power I mean power that is almost limitless and that goes unchecked. Many Western govern-ments have built in checks and balances to ensure that pure power cannot be created or achieved. Many people reading this book are probably saying that we are a civilized and educated world. There is no way that we would let someone become a dictator – Germany and Hitler are still fresh in the minds of many. Think for a minute. Do you think the people of Germany would have ever dreamt that they would be part of an actual (functional) dictatorship responsible for the loss of millions of lives? Of course they did not nor did the people from the beginning of time. It goes against man's basic human nature of wanting and desiring autonomy. Every person desires to be a functional member of a free state. No one that I have ever come across desires to be ruled by a dictator wielding absolute power.

I believe that any country, or the entire world, can become receptive to the idea of dictatorship if certain conditions exist. The fundamental condition that must exist in every situation I believe is economic turmoil. A majority of the population must be experiencing some form of financial hardship; after all, "money is what makes the world go around". There must be a desire for change. Cognitively, no one would desire a change to a dictatorship but a desire for political change must be present. The benefits of centralized power must be shown to out weight the benefits of decentralized power. Finally, you must have a person who wants to be the peoples' leader in a centralized power structure. If all of these conditions are present then the potential of seeing the creation of centralized power becomes greatly increased.

If the political, social, and economic trends continue as they exist presently, I believe that the above conditions for the potential of creating centralized power dictatorship will become present in the very near future. Once centralized power is created it is very hard for it to be "neutralized". A dictator understanding the nuances of dictatorship can help extend his centralized power by ensuring that economic wealth is more evenly distributed throughout a society than would be given another system such as democratic capitalism. Thus, if a dictatorship is created in the future you probably will see a massive redistribution of wealth. I will make the assumption that a person able to grab hold of world power will have above-average intelligence thus an understanding of the nuances of a dictatorship.

A dictatorship most likely will come to an end when the same conditions exist that existed at the time of the creation of the dictatorship; no matter how smart a dictator may be, it is impossible for any mortal man to control the world, as man is unpredictable. **Always remember that today's friend can be tomorrow's foe.**

Analysis of "Route to Dictatorship".

On the Y-axis is the intensity of the particular trend being analyzed. On the X-axis is the time in years. It seems clear that societal or world economic, social, and political trends are created over years rather than weeks or months.

Let's first examine the trend lines that intersect line b. It can be seen that there is a high intensity for a person that wants to be a leader in a centralized power structure. It can also be seen that there is a moderate desire for change. At this time the benefits of centralized power are not being made clear to the public.

Up to this point, one may make an argument that there is potential for bringing in a centralized power structure. I would have to point out that we have yet to analyze the most critical factor – poor economic conditions are very low or, in other words, economic conditions are relatively good. Given this scenario, I would have to say that the potential for bringing in centralized power is next to none.

Let us now look at the intersection of trend lines with line A. Economic conditions are very poor as indicated by a high intensity. There is also a high intensity for a person wanting to lead a centralized power structure. And there is a moderate/high intensity for the desire of change. At the same time there is only a low/moderate intensity attached to the benefits of centralized power. People are still not clear on what the benefits would actually be.

Since three out of the four key elements are close to the high intensity position on the scale and very poor economic conditions prevail, chances are that this society would adopt a more centralized power structure if the benefits could be shown to them.

Our society, for that matter, our world, is moving closer to line a!

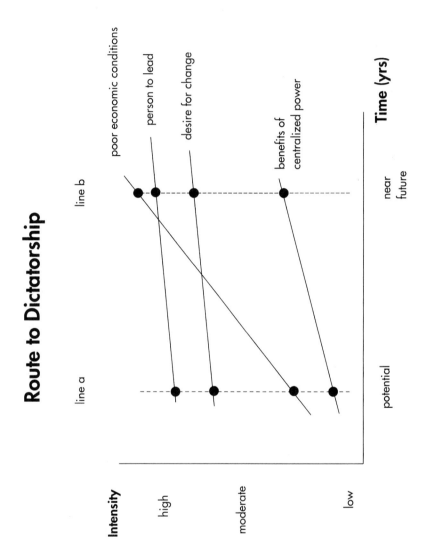

Route to Dictatorship

A Materialistic World

I am afraid that when we come through the upcoming bad years, society will become even more materialistic. The reason behind this is that people are going to lose their entire lifetime savings, investments, RRSP's, and so on. This money will be gone. No benefit will have been derived through a savings mentality. After getting nothing, even though people worked at saving money, people are going to be more likely to spend, acquiring material goods so that a loss will not happen again. I envision a general obsession by society to regain the lost material wealth and goods. Any political entity who will help achieve this will attain great power. This is the opposite of what happened to those who lived through the depression of the thirties, but society has greatly changed since then; the mentality after the depression was to save and hoard just in case the same thing happened again.

As man became more technically advanced, man's ability to 'grow' morally has not kept up at all. It is man's technical achievements which have led us to a materialistic world. When people worked on the family farm, early in the century, materialism was not very prevalent. People did not have to "keep up with the Joneses". For the most part, people were basically equal. Nobody, except for the elite, lived a life of luxury. Rather it was a life of hard work and sacrifices.

Today, tens of millions of people are in the pursuit of material goods which they believe will bring them the 'desired' happiness. This is mostly a myth. The actual reality is that the 'craving' for more and more material items often causes great pain. There are those people who are compulsive shoppers. It is like an addiction; they simply cannot stop even though they are aware of negative repercussions which they will have to face as a result of their actions. There are different degrees of intensity of this addiction. Some people will shop and shop until total financial collapse. This often includes the family house. Others will shop to the point where their entire pay cheque goes to servicing the debt incurred through this addiction.

Then others may simply buy things that are not needed and which they will eventually throw out without putting themselves in financial jeopardy.

Point of Sale Gratification

The materialistic addiction is much like drug addiction. The materialistically-addicted person feels a high at the point of purchase then feels badly and/or guilty soon after. The drug addict is the same. They both require a 'fix' to get high but soon return to the generated state of reality. Again, like a drug addict, the materialistically addicted person goes through tremendous withdrawal symptoms, if the choice is, or is forced to be made, to do something about the addiction.

The Macro The Micro

What is good for the individual (the Micro) generally will be good for the country (the Macro). And, conversely, what is bad for the individual will be bad for the country. When governments run deficits there is a direct transfer of wealth from the poor to the rich. We have seen this before. When governments borrow money, they must pay interest on this money. More than likely, the holder of the government bonds are people of affluence in our society. These people receive interest payments from the government on the money that they have lent to the government. The interest payment comes from taxes collected by the government. The main source of tax revenues is from the middle class. Thus, money is taxed from the middle class and given to the richer citizens of the country through interest payments.

The reality is that, in the short-term, the rich will gain at the expense of the less fortunate but it is my belief that these bonds and T-bills will not be paid back by the government. Thus the tables will turn in the future and the under class will have gained somewhat, at the expense of the rich; what a change this will be. When the rich are not repaid, we will see a complete economic breakdown, thus causing untold hardship for the under class (middle class). At this point, one must really question whether the middle and under class really do gain at the expense of the rich, ever!

This is the "coming dawn".

CHAPTER 8

The Final Message

I wish you happiness and success In A World Gone Mad.

Epilogue

I sincerely hope that you have thoroughly enjoyed this book. I also hope that at a minimum it has provoked thought! This book was written in such a way that it was intended to provide you the reader with an experience! I find that most books are only designed to be read; interaction between the reader and the book does not take place.

Any comments on the book and its contents are welcome and can be forwarded to the publisher attention myself, Glenn M.J. Epps.

> Life is short and simple.
> Life is long and complicated.
> Life is really a mixture of the two.
> Life requires positive action.
> Life is truly enhanced by both the simple
> and complicated actions that you take.

APPENDIX

LETTERS

I have provided a couple of different letters that you are welcome to use as is, if you so desire. All that you will have to do is add your name and address and the person's name and address to whom they are being sent.

*****Always include your name, address and, phone number; this helps legitimize the contents of your letter*****

LETTER# 1

Dear xxxx,

I am writing you this letter as I am a very concerned citizen. I am chiefly concerned about the country's economic situation and its environment.

Spending is out of control. It has been for quite some-time. At the rate we are going *there will be no positive economic future for the children of our country.* I want you to do something about both the spending problem which our government has and about all the inefficiencies in government. I have heard about the horror stories at the Pentagon – thousands of dollars for a simple tool like a hammer. This has got to stop!

Our environment is a mess. When is talk going to be replaced with action. If we keep going like we are, we are going to face mass pollution ... mass death. As a rep-resentative of the people, I am asking you to do something about it. Complacency will no longer be tolerated.

My letter to you may sound strong – it is! The problems that we are facing are not minor. They are major and will have major devastating effects on the people of this country and around the world if we do not do something about them!

Thank You.

John Doe (Your Name)

LETTER# 2

Dear xxxx,

Time and time again, I have thought about the problems that face our great country but like most I have done nothing about it. Today is different! I am doing something about it and am going to ask you to join me!

We are all in the same boat in this country. We all face colossal economic problems and enormous environmental problems. I am growing tired of hearing our political representatives talk about the problems and what should be done. I want action!

Action is the only way that these problems are going to be brought under control. I am concerned about my future and the future for the young people of this country. I want them to have the same opportunities that I had and I want them to be proud of the country that they live in.

I am asking you to get the ball rolling, so to speak. No time is better than the present.

Thank You.

John Doe (Your Name)

Terms/Definitions **As Defined by Myself**

Demographics: The study of the various age groups in society.

Dictator: A person having extreme psychological disorders. This person typically will have a feeling of not being in control of his environment, and more than likely will have acute self-esteem problems. A person who seeks to control multiple environments on a grand scale.

Distortion of Reality: Any introduced factor which reduces the clarity of understanding of any particular issue or item.

Dynamic: A changing or altering state.

Equilibrium: Any state of complete balance between any number of variables.

Euphoria: The feeling of well-being.

Fiat currency: Any currency that is not backed fully by gold reserves of a country.

Goal Congruence: Multiple plans that co-ordinate in order to achieve a much larger plan.

Goal Incongruence: Multiple plans which are all stand-alones. The individual plans do not co-ordinate in order to achieve a much larger plan.

Hierarchy: An organized structure, with organized forms of communication.

Ideology: A fundamental idea or belief.

Inflation: Too much money chasing to few goods; an erosion of the spending power of a dollar.

Macro: Any thing or any item discussed on the larger scale.

Micro: Any thing or any item discussed on a smaller scale.

Mutually Exclusive: Separate events that do not enhance one another.

Mutually Inclusive: Separate events that accentuate one another.

Natural State of Reality: A theoretical state in which utopia is achieved, by way of having no distortions of reality.

Nemesis: A just reward.

Nucleus: The central core of something. Substance is built around the nucleus.

Number Graph: A set of numbers to be analyzed. When analyzed one may or may not determine a sequence that means something to them.

Perceptual Power: The ability to have an understanding of future events/trends.

Perverse Investment: Any investment that erodes one's financial net worth.

Pro-active: Any planning done in advance of learning about a situation. Planning done before learning about event 'x'.

Re-active: Planning done after the fact. A plan that is made after learning about event 'x'.

Real Interest Rates: The advertised interest rate minus the current inflation rate.

Self-Actualization: A state whereby a person has met all required needs to survive, and has now been able to actualize needs that contribute directly to a feeling of well-being.

Spinoffs: Unanticipated benefits gained through the research of a specific idea.

Transfer Payments: The movement of money from areas of more wealth concentration to areas of lesser wealth concentration.

Utopia: A state of perfect harmony, balance and equilibrium.

Wealth Disparity: An economic situation whereby one group of people will be extremely wealthy and at the same time, there will be another group of people who are average to poor.

Widgets: A name used in order to denote some sort of product being produced.

Introspection: To look honestly at oneself and do self-criticism.

Actual Reality: A true given situation. An issue minus vested interests and spins.

Spin: to change an issue so that it more closely matches one's own needs and purposes.

Purchase/Pay Law: A fundamental ideology that requires goods/services to be paid for shortly after the purchase of such goods/services.

Black Hole: A negative situation that grows larger and larger and continually sucks the perimeter area into it.

Awareness Programs: Programs that help to educate people about actual reality.

Cautious Assertion: A statement made that questions a supposed legitimized situation or result.

Thalidomide: A drug once used to help increase fertility in women but not longer used because of terrible side effects caused to fetuses.

Stagflation: an economic situation whereby a country experiences both high inflation and high unemployment at the same time.

Strategic Planning: Long-term planning, typically over five years.

Tangible Assets: Physical pieces of property.

Epps Forecasting Method (E.F.M.): A forecasting method based
upon the premise of using actual reality.

Spin Doctor: A person hired to change the appearance and meaning of a particular issue making it better suit the needs of a person or group.

U.S. READERS

If You've Enjoyed

"Distortions of Reality"

. . . why not share it with your friends?

As a reader of this book you may order additional copies to give to your friends as gifts at a very special reduced price.

The regular price is $19.95 US per copy, but your special reduced price is only $32.00 US for two copies.

Please send your cheque or money order for $32.00 US plus $3.00 for shipping and handling, along with your name address and phone number to:
Sunrise Publishing, Suite 169, 402 Pine Avenue,
Niagara Falls, N.Y., 14301

Attn., Special Offer Department
This is a high-quality book and should last for years to come.

CANADIAN READERS

If You've Enjoyed

"Distortions of Reality"

. . . why not share it with your friends?

As a reader of this book you may order additional
copies to give to your friends as gifts at a
very special reduced price.

The regular price is $22.95 Cdn. per copy, but
your special reduced price is only $37.00 Cdn. for
two copies.

Please send your cheque or money order for $37.00 Cdn.
plus $3.00 for shipping and handling, along with your
name address and phone number to:
Sunrise Publishing, Westford Plaza, R.P.O. 2131,
Lawrence Ave. E., Box 83001, Scarborough, Ont. M1R 5G5
Attn., Special Offer Department.

This is a high-quality book and should last for years to come.

QUANTITY SALES

Sunrise Publishing books are available at special discounts when purchased in bulk by corporations, organizations, and special-interest groups. Custom imprinting or excerpting can also be done to fit special needs. For details write our head office:

Sunrise Publishing Westford Plaza R.P.O., 2131 Lawrence Ave. E., P.O. Box 83001, Scarborough, Ont., Canada, M1R 5G5 Attn.: Quantity Sales Department

I wish to say thanks to ...

Colin Kusano
Beverly Lehman

INDEX

(H) – Heading in the book

A Perspective of Two Great Countries (H), 90
Abortions, 40
AIDS, 25, 59, 129
An Expert? (H), 139
Australia, 66, 151
Awareness Programs (H), 56
Bankruptcies - The Family Farm (H), 62
Bay Street, 112
Bennett, 88
Black Hole, 53, 98
British Columbia, 121
California, 121, 128
Canada (H), 91
Canada and The United States at the Crossroads (H), 159
Capitalism (H), 74
Centralized Power the Route to Dictatorship (H), 161
Certificates of Deposits/Bonds (H), 136
Changing Weather Patterns (H), 68
Children as an Extension of an Adult (H), 39
China (H), 150
Coming Cashless Society, The (H), 57
Coming Economic Depression, The (H), 100
Coming Social Depression, The (H), 128
Constitution, 47, 49, 82, 84, 92
Corporate America Meltdown (H), 103
Czechoslovakia, 70
Deficit, 89, 96, 98-99, 109-110, 113-114, 132, 159, 164
Depression, 97, 99, 103, 136
Determination of Reality (H), 25
Diagram/Chart Index, 29, 31, 33, 55, 81, 86, 97, 147, 155, 157, 164
Divorce (H) 37-39
Donald Trump, 110
Drugs, Drugs, Drugs (H), 41
E.F.M., 141, 143
Earthquakes (H), 121
Economic Time Bomb (H), 95
Elite, 22, 43, 74, 76, 82, 165
Emotion vs Logic (H), 17
England, 83
Environment, The (H), 69
Equilibrium, 52, 63, 87
Europe, 66, 92, 144, 151
Family, The (H), 144
Father (H), 116
Fiat Currency, 106, 118, 134
Field of Economics, The (H), 94

Index

Financial Advisor, 132-133
George Bush, 61, 75, 82, 95-96, 141, 142,144
Gold as an Investment (H), 134
Gold Stocks (H), 136
Gold, 108, 117, 134-137
Government Interference (H), 77
Government Job - Welfare Recipient (H), 45
Great Depression, 88, 100, 101
Greenhouse Effect, 65
Greenpeace, 72
Gulf States, 151
Hitler, 161
Hoover, 88
I'll Do as I Please (H), 47
Industrial Revolution, 21
Inflation (H), 105
Inflation - A Closer Look (H), 109
Injustice of Justice, The (H), 43
Institutions (H), 23
Interest Rates (H), 104
Is there a Hidden Agenda (H), 113
Israel, 151
Japan, 100, 121, 145-148, 151, 161
Joe Clark, 84
John Crow, 113
Joke is on You, Unfortunately, The (H), 117
Junk Bond, 111
Lobbyists, 88
Long Term Trends (H), 156
Macro, The Micro, The (H), 166
Marriage, 35-38, 40
Materialistic World, A (H), 165
Matrix, 64
Me, Myself and I, 30
Me/I (H), 35, 40, 52
Me/I - Priority Maps, (H) 27
Middle East, The (H), 150-152
Mulroney, 89, 95-96
My Thought (H), 127
Nemisis, The (H), 51
New Age Movement, 69
New World Order, 61, 69, 103, 136, 152-153
New World Order, A (H), 152
OPEC, 152
Other Stocks (H), 136
Palestine Liberation Organization, 151
Paper Money, 117
Pay-as-you-go, 51, 112
Personal/Consumer Loans (H), 137
Perverse Investments, 108, 133
Point of Sale Gratification (H), 166

Political Democracy (H), 74
Political Economic Processes (H), 88
Preparing Yourself (H), 124
Price Leader, 111
Public Sector, The (H), 112
Purchase/Pay Law, 51
Quebec, 91
Reagan, 50, 75, 82, 95-96, 141, 142, 144, 160
Reason to Worry (H), 61
Redistribution of Wealth (H), 76
Retirement, 18
Robert Campeau, 110
Russia, 74-75, 118, 148-149
Schizophrenic, 129
Scientist, Friend or Foe?, The (H), 62
Second World War, 89
Secret of Economic Depression Unveiled, The (H), 121
Sex in Today's Society, (H), 40
Short Term Trends (H), 154
Silver (H), 136
Society (H), 52
Society's Blunder (H), 48
Some Cold Hard Realities (Facts) About Our World's Environment (H), 60
Special Interest Groups, 25, 48, 49, 50, 51, 56
Spiral of Destruction (H), 99
State of Deterioration, A (H), 132
Strategic Planning, 45, 98
Systems of Government (H), 83
Tangible Assets, 103, 118
Tax Revolt, 128
Thalidomide, 62
The Natural State of Reality (H), 20
The United States of America (H), 90
Third World, 71, 101, 120
Trends (H), 153
Truth About our Food, The (H), 63
United Nations, 70, 158
Unrecognized Step Fendly, The (H), 84
Wall Street, 112
Wealth Dispersity, 76
Weather, A Forecast of Danger, The, 65
Welfare Recipient - Government Job (H), 46
What Do I See for The Future? (H), 140
When Chaos Hits (H), 124
Who is Conning Who? (H), 42
Worker 'Pays' the Price, The (H), 105
Working Inflation (H), 106
World Powers (H), 144
Yuppie Kids, 39

Actual Reality*
"For our Times" *

Today we live in a world gone mad! There are so many complex issues to deal with. Issues that are given a spin by this person, that person, that group, or even by a hired spin doctor. These issues become distorted and contorted over and over again. Through no fault of their own everyday citizens become confused, loss sight of actual reality, and are not even aware of it.

How can a person truly prosper in a world filled with mis-information? How can a person be properly informed about current issues? Will a person understand how he is being affected by events on the other side of the world? There are so many questions to be answered. Things can be easier. All these questions can be answered in one simple way - subscribe to *Actual Reality.*

Actual Reality informs the reader about different timely economic, social, political and environmental issues. Today, more than at any other time in history, it is important to understand what is actually going on around you.

Exciting and revealing quarterly publications of Actual Reality take complicated issues and makes them understandable so that you can make informed decisions. When things really get chaotic, ultra-dynamic special editions of Actual Reality keep you informed. Living without *Actual Reality* means living in a Distortion of Reality.

→ Editor and Chief of *Actual Reality* is Glenn M.J. Epps. ←

Don't delay subscribe today! A one-year quarterly subscription to Actual Reality is being offered at the incredibly low price of only $12.95 US / $14.95 CDN, including postage and handling. Send your cheque or money order to Sunrise Publishing, Station A, Box 83001, 2131 Lawrence Ave. E., Scarborough, Ont., M1R 5G5

* Trademarks of Sunrise Publishing